OAXACA VALLEY

JUSTIN HENDERSON

Contents

Oaxaca City ... 5
Planning Your Time ... 10

Sights ... 11
Orientation ... 11
Around the *Zócalo* ... 11
Northwest of the *Zócalo* ... 13
Andador Macedonio Alcalá ... 14
Los Arquitos ... 18

Entertainment and Events ... 19
Around the *Zócalo* ... 19
Festivals ... 19
Arts Events ... 21
Nightlife ... 22

Sports and Recreation ... 24
Mountain Biking ... 24
Horseback Riding ... 24
Swimming, Tennis, and Golf ... 25
Walking ... 25

Shopping ... 25
Traditional Markets ... 26
Private Handicrafts Shops ... 26
Clothing and Textiles ... 27
Fine Art galleries ... 28
Curiosity Shops ... 28
Cutlery and Metalwork Shops ... 29
Sporting Goods and Clothes ... 29

Accommodations ... 29
Near the *Zócalo* ... 30
North and East of the *Zócalo* ... 31
South and West of the *Zócalo* ... 36
Apartments ... 36
Hostels ... 37
Trailer Parks and Camping ... 37

Food ... 38
Around the *Zócalo* ... 38
North of the *Zócalo* ... 39
South of the *Zócalo* ... 42

Information and Services ... 44
Tourist Information ... 44
Health and Emergencies ... 45
Bookstores and Publications ... 45

Money Exchange.....................46	Teotitlán del Valle.....................61
Communications.....................46	Tlacolula.............................63
Libraries............................46	Yagul Archaeological Zone...........65
Consulates and Immigration..........47	Mitla................................65
Laundry.............................47	Hierve El Agua......................68
Photography........................47	
Volunteer Work and Donations........47	**The Crafts Route**.............70
Language Instruction and Courses....47	San Bartolo Coyotepec...............70
Oaxacan Cooking and Culture.........48	San Martín Tilcajete and Santo Tomás Jalieza................72
Transportation................48	Ocotlán.............................72
Air..................................48	San Sebastián de las Grutas..........73
Car or RV...........................49	Southwest Side......................75
Van.................................51	**Monte Albán and**
Bus.................................51	**the Archaeological**
The Valley	**Route**...........................77
of Oaxaca...................54	Monte Albán.........................77
Planning Your Time..................58	Santa María Atzompa................82
Getting Around......................58	
The Textile Route............59	
El Tule and Tlacochahuaya...........59	
Dainzu and Lambityeco Archaeological Sites...............60	

Oaxaca City

Sights 11	Accommodations. 29
Entertainment and Events 19	Food 38
Sports and Recreation 24	Information and Services 44
Shopping. 25	Transportation. 48

Highlights

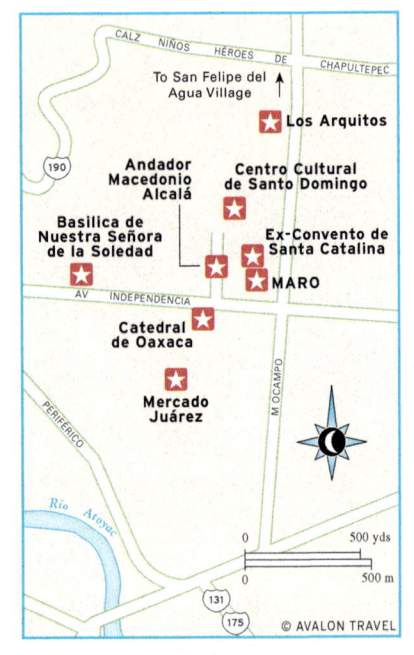

★ **Basilica de Nuestra Señora de la Soledad:** Five pounds of gold and 600 diamonds crown Oaxaca's adored patron, and a fascinating adjacent museum preserves her beloved legacy (page 14).

★ **Andador Macedonio Alcalá:** In the blocks surrounding the junction of the pedestrian promenade and Centro Cultural, dozens of great new bars, restaurants, galleries, and all manner of unique retail stores have opened, turning this area into the city's most vibrant neighborhood for visitors (page 14).

★ **Ex-Convento de Santa Catalina:** Wander the tranquil inner courtyards of this richly restored ex-convent, now a distinguished hotel (page 16).

★ **Centro Cultural de Santo Domingo:** Explore the celebrated duo: the art-swathed Iglesia y Ex-Convento de Santo Domingo and the adjacent Museo de las Culturas de Oaxaca, with its golden treasure of Monte Albán's Tomb 7 (page 16).

★ **Los Arquitos:** The original 18th-century aqueduct still stands in Oaxaca City's uptown northwest corner, in a quaint string of arches. The surrounding neighborhood is ripe for strolling winding village lanes and lingering at a sprinkling of shops, small cafés, and an all-natural Saturday food market (page 18).

★ **Mercado Juárez:** A regiment of stalls offers the best traditional Oaxaca merchandise, from *huipiles* to mountain-gathered remedies and spit-roasted chickens (page 11).

★ **Catedral de Oaxaca:** The restored facade and the inner chapel, which enshrines one of the four replicas of the Holy Cross of Huatulco, highlight a visit to this plaza-front gem (page 13).

★ **MARO:** Do a major part of your Oaxaca handicrafts shopping at this store, run by a remarkable group of native Oaxacan women artisans (page 26).

The city of Oaxaca (wah-HAH-kah; pop. 400,000, elev. 1,778 meters/5,110 feet) is both the governmental capital of Mexico's fifth-largest state by area (about tenth largest by population) and the de facto capital of Mexico's southern indigenous heartland. And Oaxaca is southern indeed. It lies farther south than all of Mexico's state capitals save one, Tuxtla Gutiérrez, the capital of Chiapas. Oaxaca nestles in a temperate highland valley, blessed with a year-round balmy, spring-like climate, prized by both residents and visitors.

Every year, starting in mid-July, Oaxaca City becomes the focus of the extraordinary diversity of its entire state. In the celebrated Guelaguetza (gay-lah-GAY-tzah; The Giving) festival, indigenous Oaxaca people, speaking 16 unique languages and representing hundreds of Oaxaca's ethnic groups, converge in the city for a grand two-week party of food, dancing, music, and general merrymaking.

The Guelaguetza, like virtually all of Oaxaca's civic revelries, starts at the *zócalo* (central plaza), ringed by relaxing sidewalk cafés and bordered by the porticoed Palacio de Gobierno on its south side and the distinguished baroque bulk of the Catedral de Oaxaca on its north side.

With some exceptions, this north side of Oaxaca City is more welcoming and exciting to tourists and locals alike, with most of the better new restaurants, stores, and bars located "uptown," along the pedestrian walkway known as the Andador Macedonio Alcalá (hereafter referred to as the Alcalá) and other streets such as Allende, García Vigil, and Bravo. There is plenty to do farther south, for that is where the city's great traditional markets can be found, but uptown is where most of the younger Oaxacans like to spend their time.

From the *zócalo,* the city's street grid spreads south past the town's vibrant pair of central markets, the Mercado Juárez and the Mercado San Juan de Dios, and north, uphill, along the Alcalá. The walkway connects the *zócalo* with Oaxaca's uptown monuments, most notably Oaxaca's jewel, the Centro

Previous: facade of Catedral de Oaxaca; Santo Domingo cathedral and plaza. **Above:** Museo de las Culturas de Oaxaca.

Oaxaca City

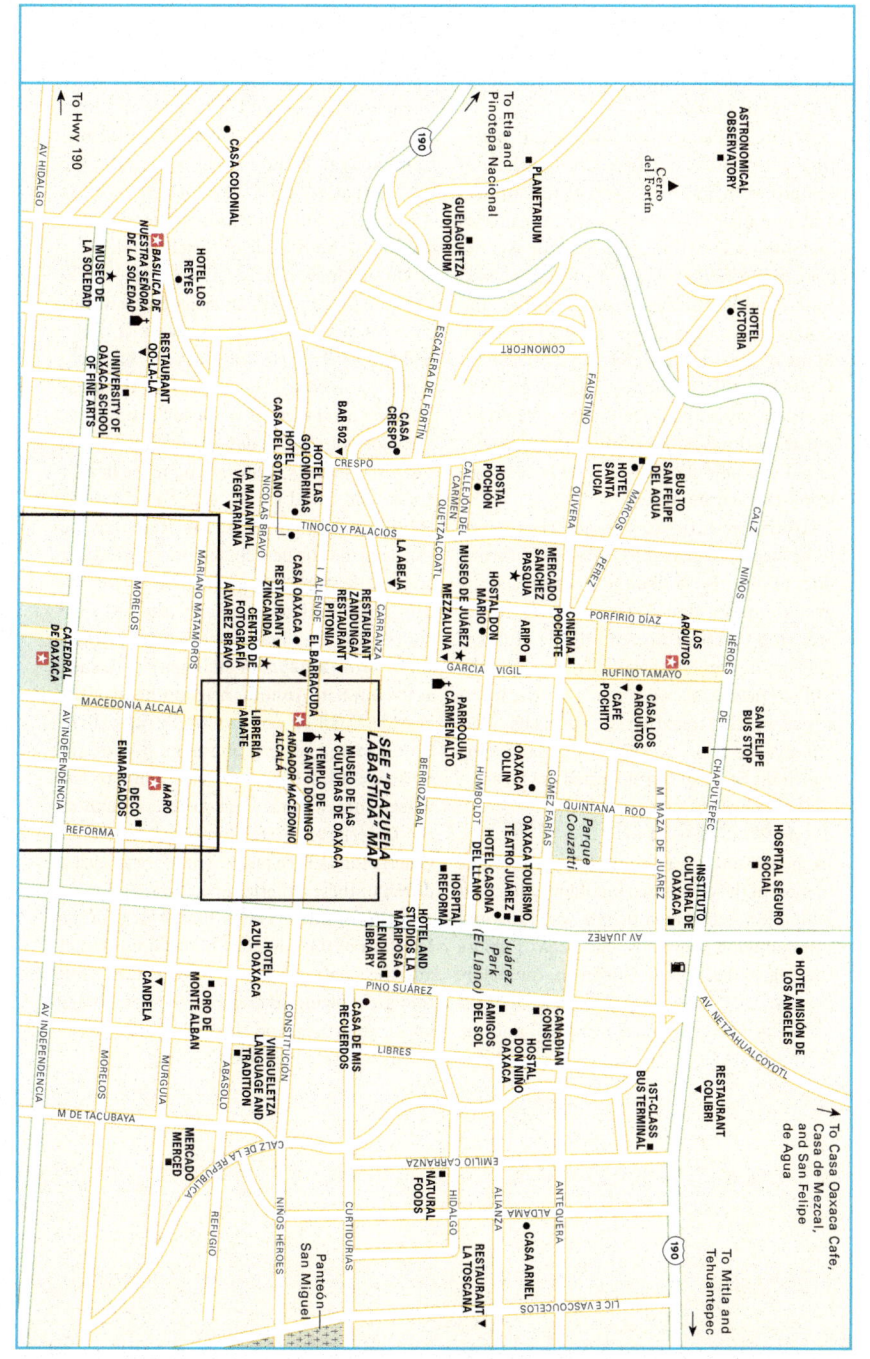

OAXACA CITY

Cultural de Santo Domingo, made up of the Iglesia y Ex-Convento de Santo Domingo and the adjacent magnificent Museo de las Culturas de Oaxaca.

Where Andador Macedonio Alcalá meets the Centro Cultural, a lively street life has developed, with dozens of bars and restaurants, and a number of contemporary art galleries and stores selling fine crafts from all over the state, beautiful jewelry, *mezcal* from myriad individual distilleries, organic coffee, and clothes, especially high-end designer fashions. Many of the designers creating these clothes synthesize colorful Oaxacan fabric and textile traditions with contemporary urban style. For those looking for a hip and lively mix of old and new Oaxaca—call it Oaxacan fusion—this is ground zero.

To the west, the city streets climb even more steeply, and as the Guelaguetza throng does in July, the westbound streets reach the grand outdoor dance stage and amphiteater atop Oaxaca's storied hillside of Cerro del Fortín. This hill, originally known as the hill of Huaxyacac, was named for the forest of pod-bearing trees that still covers its slope. Huaxyacac was the city's original name, which the Spanish transliterated as Oaxaca.

PLANNING YOUR TIME

In about four fairly relaxed days, you can take in most of the downtown highlights. Start out with a leisurely day of people-watching and café-lounging around the old *zócalo*. Explore the nearby Palacio de Gobierno, the colorful **Mercado Juárez,** the baroque **Templo y Ex-Convento de San Agustín,** and the **Catedral de Oaxaca.**

Spend your second day in the multitude of shops along the **Andador Macedonio Alcalá,** at the **Museo de Arte Contemporaneo,** and in the **Ex-Convento de Santa Catalina,** now restored as the Hotel Camino Real. Be sure to enjoy lunch on the relaxing patios of the Danzantes or Hostería Alcalá restaurants. Or try one of the great new restaurants on Allende or García Vigil.

On day three, visit the **Centro Cultural de Santo Domingo,** which includes the world-class **Museo de las Culturas de Oaxaca** and the lovely **Iglesia y Ex-Convento de Santo Domingo.** Have a look at the adjacent botanical gardens while you're upstairs.

Spend your fourth day following your own interests, such as investigating more handicrafts and retail stores, especially **MARO** (Mujeres Artesanías de las Regiones de Oaxaca) and the new contemporary clothing and textile stores along Cinco de Mayo; visiting small museums, notably the **Casa de Juárez** and the **Museo Arte Prehispánico de Rufino Tamayo;** or taking in sights, such as the intimate Arquitos neighborhood or the gemlike **Basílica de Nuestra Señora de la Soledad** and adjacent museum, **Museo de la Soledad.** Alternately, visit some of the newer contemporary art galleries, such as the Galería 910 Arte Contemporaneo and Galería Linda Fernandez. There are at least a dozen of these galleries open now, and most of them are within two or three blocks of the junction of the Andador Macedonio Alcalá and the Centro Cultural. For the most part, they are showing art created by contemporary Oaxacan artists, and there are a number of artists whose work is worth seeing.

Sights

ORIENTATION

The streets of Oaxaca still run along the same simple north-south grid the city founders laid out in 1529. If you stand at the center of the old *zócalo* and look out toward the *catedral* across Avenida Hidalgo, you will be looking north. Diagonally left, to the northwest, you'll see the smaller plaza, **Alameda de León,** and directly beyond that, in the distance, the historic hill of Huayacac, now called **Cerro del Fortín.** Along the base of Cerro del Fortín, the Pan American Highway (National Highway 190) runs generally east-west through the northern suburbs.

Turn around—we're still standing in the zócalo—and you'll see the porticoed facade of the former **Palacio de Gobierno,** now a museum. This main entry side of the palacio has been occupied by radical unionists for years—their banners and billboards have taken on a wearily permanent look—but everybody has learned to live with them. If you find a clear vantage point, you'll see the hill of **Monte Albán** looming above the southwest horizon.

The venerable restored downtown buildings and streets, some converted to traffic-free promenades, make a delightful strolling ground for discovering traditional Mexico at its best. The shady old *zócalo,* officially called Jardín Juárez, basks at the heart of it all, a perfect place for taking a seat at one of many sidewalk cafés and watching the world glide by. Its portals, clockwise from the west side, are named Flores, Clavería, Juárez, and Mercaderes.

It is useful to know that almost all of the streets running east-west, and most of the north-south ones as well, change their names as they cross major arteries. For example, Calle Constitución in the northwest quadrant of downtown turns into Calle Allende as it crosses the Alcalá. And north-south Porfirio Díaz becomes 20 de Noviembre as it crosses Avenida Morelos. These name changes, which are not consistent in terms of where they happen, can take some getting used to.

AROUND THE *ZÓCALO*
Palacio de Gobierno

Give the guards a cheery *"buenos días"* or *"buenas tardes"* at the temporary entrance (the long-term occupation of the front entrance by radicals is ongoing) near southwest *zócalo* corner, on Flores Magón, of the former statehouse-now-museum **Palacio de Gobierno** (south side of the *zócalo,* 951/501-1662, 10am-7pm Mon.-Sat., 10am-5pm Sun., $2), and step inside. City fathers first built a city hall on the same site in 1576. Repeated earthquakes led to reconstructions, until 1948, when the present building, a modernized and strengthened version of the previous 1884 structure, was finished.

Inside, you'll find a beautifully renovated museum, highlighted by dramatic historic murals by Arturo Bustos in the stairwell area, and an excellent 2nd-floor science and natural history sub-museum. In the center of the Bustos mural is Oaxaca's favorite son and Mexico's revered *presidente,* Benito Juárez, and his wife, Margarita Maza.

★ Mercado Juárez

The traditional **Juárez market** (most shops open by 8am and close by 6pm daily) occupies the one-block square that begins just one block south and one block west of the *zócalo.* Dozens of stalls offer traditional Oaxaca merchandise—such as dresses, *huipiles,* woven blankets, serapes, and herbs.

While at the market, be sure to step to the southwest corner of 20 de Noviembre and Rayón for a history lesson in art inside the **Templo y Ex-Convento de San Juan de Dios,** which stands on the site of Oaxaca's oldest church. The present structure, completed in 1703, replaced the former earthquake-damaged 1535 town cathedral, which

Downtown Oaxaca City

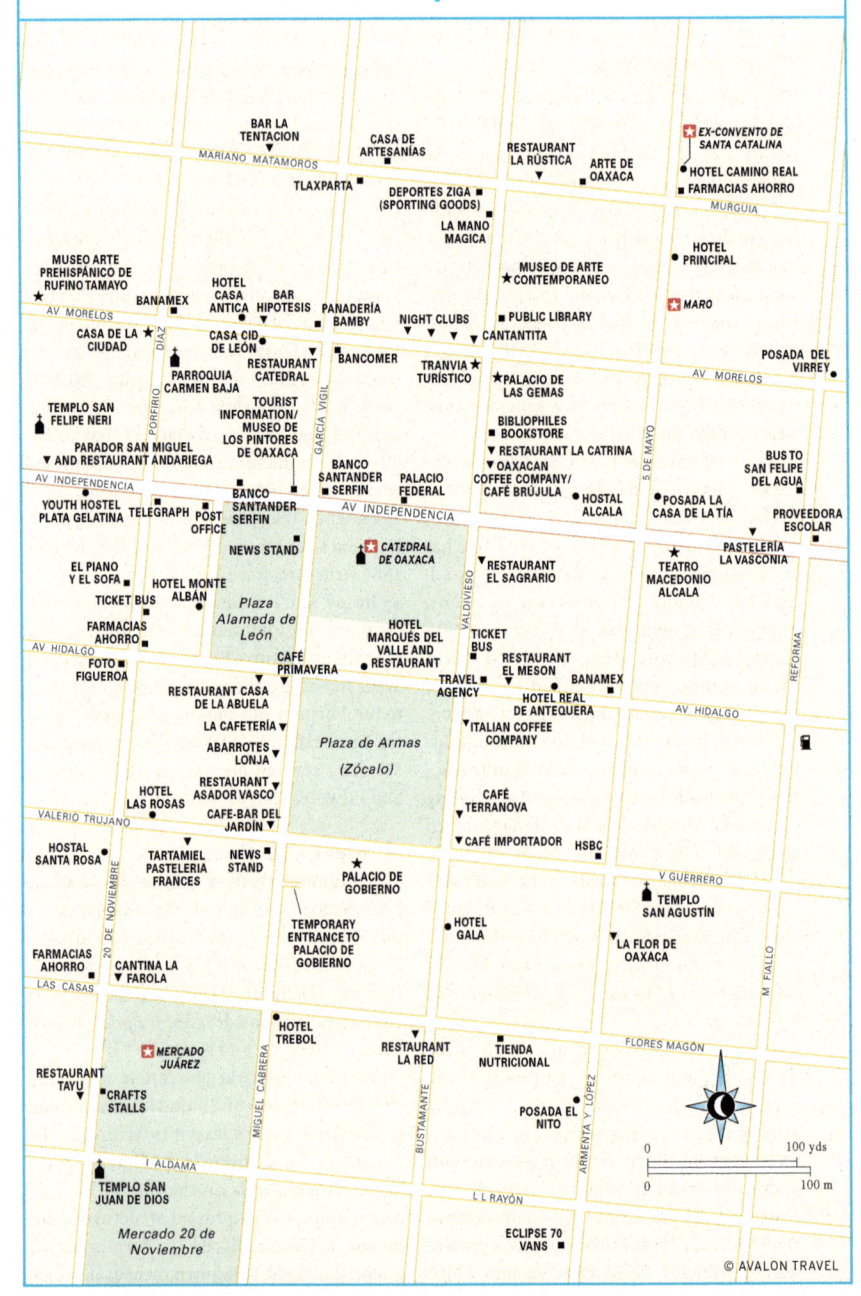

itself replaced the original 1521 adobe structure. Large, luminous paintings lining the nave walls depict landmarks in Oaxaca's religious history.

Templo y Ex-Convento de San Agustín

Off-*zócalo* side streets are studded with Oaxaca's old church gems. One of the most precious and most accessible is the **San Agustín church and ex-convent** (on Calle Guerrero), one block due east from the Palacio de Gobierno. One of the few Oaxacan works of the Augustinian order, the original adobe church on this site was finished in 1596, but it was seriously damaged by subsequent earthquakes. The present church, finished in 1722, replaced the original.

★ Catedral de Oaxaca

Return to the *zócalo*'s north side for a look at the present cathedral. It replaced the 1550 original, demolished by an earthquake in 1696. Finished in 1733, the present cathedral is distinguished by its Greek-marble main altar, where a polished Italian bronze Virgin of the Ascension is being drawn upward to the cloud-tipped heavenly domain of the Holy Spirit (the dove) and God (the sunburst).

Of considerable historical interest is the **Santa Cruz de Huatulco** (Holy Cross of Huatulco), enshrined in a chapel at the middle, south (right) side of the nave. The cross, about two feet high, in the glass case atop the chapel altar, is one of four made in 1612 by Oaxaca bishop Juan Cervantes from the original mysterious cross worshipped by the natives on the southern Oaxaca coast long before the conquest. An explanation, in Spanish, gives three versions of the story of the cross, which, as the natives reported to the conqueror Pedro Alvarado in 1522, was erected long before by a strange, white-robed holy man who soon departed and never returned. Bishop Cervantes sent the three other copies of the cross, respectively, to authorities at Santa María Huatulco municipality, Mexico City, and Rome.

NORTHWEST OF THE *ZÓCALO*
Templo de San Felipe Neri

Just two blocks west of Catedral de Oaxaca rises the distinguished facade of the **Templo de San Felipe Neri** (on Independencia, corner of Tinoco and Palacios, open for worship 8am-11pm daily). The building is immediately notable, for it faces south, unlike the great

herbal remedies for sale, Mercado Juárez

majority of Oaxaca's churches, which follow tradition and face west.

Its builders finished the structure, once a convent of the order of San Felipe Neri, and dedicated it to the Virgin of Patrocinio in 1773. The subsequent 1795 earthquake caused extensive damage, which was not completely repaired until the 20th century. Unfortunately, more earthquakes, in 1928 and 1931, inflicted additional destruction. The present restoration was completed in 1985.

Museo Arte Prehispánico de Rufino Tamayo

Just one block farther north, **Museo Arte Prehispánico de Rufino Tamayo** (503 Morelos, tel. 951/516-4750, 10am-2pm and 4pm-7pm Mon. and Wed.-Sat., 10am-3pm Sun., $3) exhibits the brilliant pre-Columbian artifact collection of celebrated artist Rufino Tamayo (1899-1991). Displays include hosts of animal motifs—Colima dogs, parrots, ducks, snakes—whimsically crafted into polychrome vases, bowls, and urns.

★ Basílica de Nuestra Señora de la Soledad

Continue three blocks west, past the University of Oaxaca School of Fine Arts and the airy Plaza of Dances, to the baroque **Basílica de Nuestra Señora de la Soledad** (Calle Morelos, at the Plaza de las Danzas, tel. 951/516-5076, 9am-2pm and 4pm-6pm daily, free admission). Inside, the Virgen de la Soledad (Virgin of Solitude), the patron of Oaxaca, stands atop the altar with her five-pound solid golden crown, encrusted with 600 diamonds.

Step into the **Museo de la Soledad** (Calle Morelos, at the Plaza de las Danzas, tel. 951/516-5076, 9am-2pm and 4pm-6pm daily, free admission) at the downhill side of the church, on the rear end. A multitude of objects of adornment, including shells, paintings, and jewelry, crowd cabinets, shelves, and aisles of musty rooms.

the Basílica de Nuestra Señora de la Soledad

★ ANDADOR MACEDONIO ALCALÁ

The **Andador Macedonio Alcalá** pedestrian mall, named after the composer of the Oaxacan hymn "Dios Nunca Muere" ("God Never Dies"), leads north from the *zócalo*. Paved with Oaxaca green stone in 1985 and freed of auto traffic one block north of the *zócalo*, the mall connects the *zócalo* with a number of not-to-be-missed Oaxaca sights.

The neighborhood around Andador Macedonio Alcalá is now home to a colorful assortment of crafts and clothing stores, bars, restaurants, and art galleries. You'll find a lineup of galleries on Calle Gurrión, by the Santa Domingo plaza, and around the corner on Cinco de Mayo. These galleries feature the work of contemporary Oaxacan artists, and much of it is world-class. However, exploring the retail clothing stores on Cinco de Mayo and the Andador itself can be even more intriguing. It is here that Oaxacan designers are reinventing the Oaxacan traditions—textiles

Around Andador Macedonio Alcalá

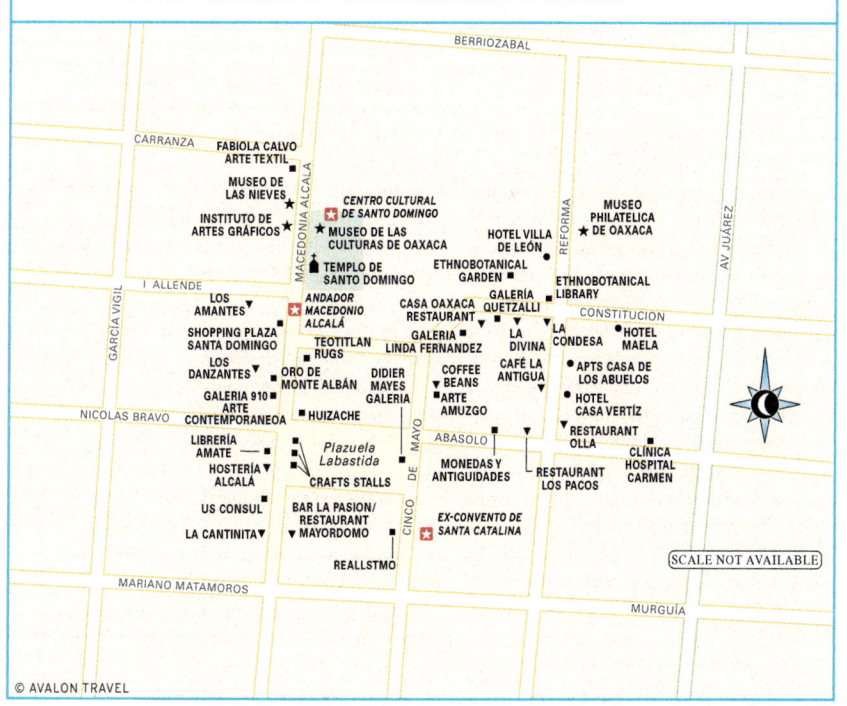

and styles of clothing—for contemporary women and men. There are also half a dozen great restaurants nearby, where a new wave of chefs is doing the same for food what the designers are doing for threads. There are also bars for every kind of drinker, from late-night rock and roll dives to tiny little rooms devoted to a particular, and particularly refined and flavorful, brand of *mezcal*.

Teatro Alcalá

Christened by a 1909 opening performance of *Aida*, the **Teatro Alcalá** (900 Independencia, tel. 951/516-8312 or 951/516-8344, 9am-5pm Mon.-Fri., admission free, except during events) houses a treasury of Romantic-era art. Above the foyer, a sumptuous marble staircase rises to a bas-relief medallion allegorizing the triumph of art. Inside, soaring above the orchestra, a heavenly choir of muses, representing the arts, decorates the ceiling.

To get to the theater from the back of the Catedral de Oaxaca head right one block along Independencia to the corner of Independencia and Cinco de Mayo.

Museo de Arte Contemporaneo de Oaxaca

Continuing north along Andador Macedonio Alcalá past the bookstore (which sells some English-language history, art, and travel books), you soon reach the **Museo de Arte Contemporaneo de Oaxaca** (Macedonio Alcalá 202, tel. 951/514-1055, www.museo-maco.com, 10am-6pm daily, free admission). Exhibitions feature works of local and nationally known modern artists.

For a change of pace, enjoy an airy

45-minute ride around town on the motorized trolley **Tranvia Turístico** (corner of Macedonio Alcalá and Morelos, $3 pp), which takes off hourly, half a block downhill from the Museo de Arte Contemporaneo.

★ Ex-Convento de Santa Catalina

Continue uphill and, at Murguia, detour right again, to the **Ex-Convento de Santa Catalina** (Cinco de Mayo 600, tel. 951/516-0611, public tours 5pm Tues.-Fri., free), the second-oldest women's convent in New Spain, founded in 1576. Although the quarters of the first novitiates were spare, the convent grew into a sprawling chapel and cloister complex decorated by fountains and flower-strewn gardens. Juárez's reforms drove the sisters out in 1862; the building has since served as city hall, school, and movie theater. Now it stands beautifully restored as the Hotel Camino Real. Note the native-motif original murals that the renovation revealed on interior walls.

★ Centro Cultural de Santo Domingo

Return to the Andador Macedonio Alcalá and continue another block uphill to Oaxaca's pride, the **Centro Cultural de Santo Domingo** (corner of Macedonio Alcalá and I. Allende, tel. 951/516-2991 or 951/516-3721, free admission), which contains two main parts, side by side: the Museo de las Culturas de Oaxaca and the Iglesia y Ex-Convento de Santo Domingo, both behind the broad Plaza Santo Domingo maguey garden and pedestrian square.

Inside, the **Iglesia y Ex-Convento de Santo Domingo** (7am-1pm and 5pm-8pm daily) glows with a wealth of art. Above the antechamber spreads the entire genealogical tree of Santo Domingo de Guzmán, starting with Mother Mary and weaving through a score of noblemen and women to the saint himself over the front door. Continuing inside, the soaring, Sistine Chapel-like nave glitters with saints, cherubs, and Bible-story paintings.

Next door, the **Museo de las Culturas de Oaxaca** (10am-6:15pm Tues.-Sun., admission $4, audio tour $5) occupies the completely restored convent section of the Santo Domingo church. Exhibitions begin on the bottom floor in rooms adjacent to the massive convent cloister, restored in 1998 to all of its original austere beauty. A downstairs highlight is the long-neglected but now safely preserved **Biblioteca de Francisco Burgoa,**

The Catedral de Oaxaca looms over the city's central plaza.

which you can walk right through and examine some of the more important works on display. The earliest work in the collection of 23,000 titles is a 1484 commentary on the works of Aristotle by Juan Versor.

A Museo sign points you upstairs via a glittering, restored, towering, domed chamber, adorned overhead with the Dominican founding fathers, presided over by Santo Domingo de Guzmán himself.

The museum also includes a **jardín etno-botánico** (ethno-botanical garden; enter at northwest corner of Reforma and Constitución, tel./fax 951/516-5325 or 951/516-7915; tours in Spanish 5pm Fri. and Sat., $5 pp; tours in English 11am Sat., $10 pp) in its big backyard. The staff conducts tours regularly and there is an announced schedule, but the schedule seems to change often. Inquire (check for the tour schedule on the door) at the ethno-botanical library at the garden entrance, two blocks behind the Santo Domingo churchfront. Visitors are not allowed to explore the gardens on their own; you have to take the tour. Or, easier, observe the garden from above, from the adjacent cultural center. There are fine views, and unless you're a botanist or determined to bond with the garden, you'll probably get enough of a look.

Small Museums

Back outside, step across the Alcalá, a few doors uphill, into the rust-colored old building now restored as the museum of the **Instituto de Artes Gráficos de Oaxaca** (Macedonio Alcalá 507, tel. 951/516-6980, 10am-8pm daily, free admission). Inside, displays exhibit mostly contemporary etchings, wood-block prints, and paintings by artists of both national and international renown.

Head west one block (along the Plazuela del Carmen, off the Macedonio Alcalá across from the museum) to the **Casa de Juárez** museum (609 García Vigil, tel. 951/516-1860, 10am-7pm Tues.-Sun., $3). The modest but beautifully restored house was the home of Juárez's benefactor, priest, and bookbinder: Father Antonio Salanueva.

Later, if you have time, return to the Santo Domingo church plaza and continue east past the church along Constitución to the **Museo Filatelia de Oaxaca** (Reforma 504, just uphill from the corner of Constitución, tel. 951/514-2366 or 951/514-8028, www.mufi.org.mx, 10am-8pm Tues.-Sun., $2). This elegant, little, modern museum displays the noted collection of José Cosino y Cosio—a library of international postal paraphernalia—and other postal-themed artworks. It's a surprisingly engaging institution.

the library of Franicisco Burgoa in the Museo de las Culturas de Oaxaca

Return a block and a half down Reforma and turn right at Abasolo, which, past Macedonio Alcalá, becomes M. Bravo. Continue a block to the **Centro de Fotografía Manuel Alvarez Bravo** (M. Bravo 116, corner of García Vigil, tel. 951/516-9800, 9am-8pm Wed.-Mon., free admission). Galleries display the work of both locally prominent and internationally acclaimed photographers, while instructors in classrooms conduct photography classes for children, adult beginners, and professionals.

Back downhill, at the north edge of the *zócalo* stands a regally restored colonial-era house, formerly the Oaxaca state tourism headquarters, now home to the **Museo de los Pintores Oaxaqueños** (Museum of Oaxacan Painters; corner of Independencia and García Vigil, tel. 951/516-5645, 10am-6pm Tues.-Sun., $2, free Sun.). It houses an eclectic, revolving collection of modern art on two floors around a central patio. Presently, the state *Turismo* agency maintains a tourist information desk to the left as you enter the museum.

★ LOS ARQUITOS

Long ago, Oaxaca's city founders provided for a permanent local water supply. They tapped the bountiful natural springs flowing from the mountains rising directly north of the city, topped by the towering Cerro San Felipe (elev. 3,100 meters/10,200 feet). The aqueduct they built gave rise to the name San Felipe del Agua, the foothill village where the aqueduct begins. Although now replaced by underground steel pipes, the original 18th-century aqueduct still stands, paralleling the downhill road from San Felipe and ending in a quaint string of arches, called **Los Arquitos,** in the city neighborhood several blocks northwest of Iglesia y Ex-Convento de Santo Domingo.

Walking Tour

The following is a one- or two-hour stroll through the relatively close-in Los Arquitos neighborhood.

Starting from the Santo Domingo churchfront, at the corner of Macedonio Alcalá and Allende, walk north, uphill along Macedonio Alcalá three blocks to Humboldt. Turn left and continue two blocks to busy Porfirio Díaz, where, across the street rises a towering fig tree that marks the **Mercado Sánchez Pasqua.** Continue past the tree to the entrance of the market. Inside, you'll first find dry goods, clothes,

Los Arquitos

and handicrafts shops, and then a mix of colorful fruit and vegetable stalls. Soon you'll arrive at the *fondas* (food stalls), for which Mercado Sánchez Pasqua is famous. Here you can enjoy a homestyle breakfast or a special lunch treat.

Retrace your steps back outside, across Porfirio Díaz, to Humboldt one block and turn left at García Vigil. Continue north to the corner of Calle Xolotl (show-LOH-tuhl), where García Vigil changes to Calle Rufino Tamayo. Pass (on the left, above the street), the art-film **Cinema El Pochote** (García Vigil 817, tel. 951/514-1194, films at 6pm and 8pm Tues.-Sat.).

Continue uphill along Tamayo, paralleling the arches for three blocks, until you reach busy east-west thoroughfare Calzada Niños Héroes. Don't miss the little shrine built beneath one arch, at Tamayo 802, and also the tiny café, El Pavito (The Little Peacock), beneath another. Be sure to explore some of the side lanes, such as the one opposite Tamayo 818 that heads beneath an arch and opens into a tiny plaza presided over by Archangel Gabriel.

Entertainment and Events

AROUND THE *ZÓCALO*

The Oaxaca *zócalo*, years ago relieved of traffic, is ideal ground for spontaneous or unexpected diversions, such as the young American modern dance troupe and their Oaxacan students who put on a sterling performance in the middle of the zócalo in a rainstorm in June 2014. Such events transpire all the time, I'm told. Regular concerts serenade from the *zócalo* band kiosk beginning around 6pm virtually every evening: the Oaxaca state band, Tuesday and Thursday; Marimba band, Wednesday (at 6:30pm); and the Oaxaca orchestra, Sunday. Furthermore, the Oaxaca state band also plays Wednesdays and Saturdays, at noon. (Schedules may change; verify with Oaxaca state tourism, 703 Av. Juárez, tel. 951/516-0123.)

FESTIVALS

There seems to be a festival somewhere in the Valley of Oaxaca every week of the year. Oaxaca's wide ethnic diversity explains much of the celebrating. Each of the groups celebrates its own traditions. Sixteen languages, in dozens of dialects, are spoken within the state. Authorities recognize around 500 distinct regional costumes.

The Guelaguetza

All of this ethnic ferment focuses in the city during the July **Lunes del Cerro** (Mondays on the Hill) festival, so named because it kicks off on the first Monday following July 16—the **Día de la Virgen de Carmen** (Virgin of Carmen day)—and continues for two weeks, when Oaxaca City is awash with both travelers, and native Oaxacans in costume from all seven traditional regions of the state.

This gathering was known in pre-Hispanic times as the **Guelaguetza** (gay-lah-GAY-tzah, or "offering"), a time of feasting, when tribes reunited for rituals and dancing in honor of Centeotl, the god of corn. The ceremonies, which climaxed with the sacrifice of a virgin who had been fed hallucinogenic mushrooms, were changed to tamer, mixed Christian-native rites by the Catholic Church. Lilies replaced marigolds—the flower of death—and saints sat in for the indigenous gods.

During recent times, the Guelaguetza festival has grown to include a grand crafts exposition at the *zócalo* and an agricultural fair. Festivities climax on each of the two Mondays at the Guelaguetza dance amphitheater on the Cerro del Fortín hill northwest of the city. Thousands of spectators thrill to the whirling, stomping, and swaying performances of dozens of brightly costumed troupes, which wow the crowd by throwing offerings of fruit, candy, and handicrafts from the stage.

If you're coming, bring sunglasses and a hat for shade, and make hotel reservations several months ahead of time. Hotels customarily offer packages that include tickets (about $40) for each Guelaguetza performance. Alternatively, local Ticketmaster outlets usually sell tickets, adding a fee of about $15. For more information, contact the **Oaxaca state tourist information office** (703 Av. Juárez, tel. 951/516-0123, www.aoaxaca.com, 8am-8pm daily) on the west side of El Llano park.

Note: If the first Monday after July 16 happens to fall on July 18, the anniversary of Benito Juárez's death, the first Lunes del Cerro shifts to the succeeding Monday, July 25.

On the Sunday before the first Lunes del Cerro, Oaxacans celebrate their history and culture at the Plaza de Danzas, adjacent to the Iglesia de la Virgen de la Soledad. Events include a big sound, light, and dance show and depictions in tableaux of the four periods of Oaxaca history.

If you miss the Lunes del Cerro festival, some towns and villages stage smaller Guelaguetza celebrations year-round. A number of hotels do as well, most frequently the **Hotel Monte Albán** (Alameda de León 1, tel. 951/516-2777, usually 8:30pm daily, $7), adjacent to the *zócalo;* or most elaborately, the hotel **Camino Real** (Cinco de Mayo 300, tel. 951/516-0611, www.caminoreal.com/Oaxaca, 7pm Fri., $28 show with buffet, not including drinks). Also, **Restaurant Casa de Cantera** (on northside Calle Dr. Federico Armengal, at the top of Av. Porfirio Díaz, tel. 951/514-7585 or 951/514-9522, www.casadecantera.com, 9pm several nights a week, $15 pp, including a snack) has staged a popular Guelaguetza show for years.

Day of the Dead

Instead of mourning the dead, Mexicans celebrate the deceased with a holiday, **El Día de los Muertos** (The Day of the Dead), which is, in all of Mexico and especially in Oaxaca, cause for a fiesta that goes on for a week and culminates with the three days that comprise El Día de los Muertos. Some say that this holiday, which takes place from October 31 to November 2, should be called Día con los Muertos, for it is not so much that the dead are honored but rather that they come to visit.

The roots of this festival go back some 3,000 years, to an ancient Aztec festival dedicated to Mictecacihuatl, the guardian-goddess

Steps lead down from the Guelaguetza dance amphitheater into the city.

of the dead, celebrated by pre-Hispanic Mexicans during the month of August (later moved to its current dates by the Catholics, to coincide with their own holy days of All Saints Day and All Souls Day). With its relatively intact pre-Hispanic cultures, Oaxaca celebrates this mixed indigenous and Christian holiday with more fervor, solemnity, and gaiety than any other part of Mexico.

In Oaxaca City the festivities begin a week prior to November 1, when every market spills over with all the decorations, foods, and materials required for the arrival of the dead. Flowers are gathered, especially marigolds *(cempasuchil),* and then, on October 31 and the following two days, altars are constructed in homes and plazas and countless locations. These often-elaborate altars are loaded up with aromatic foods favored by the dead: Oaxacan mole, corn jelly *(nicuatole),* pumpkin with black sugar, stone ground chocolate, and the sweet bread of the dead *(pan de muerto).* Fruits are also heaped on the altars. Candles are placed and lit, and marigolds are added as the final decorative touch, all over the altars and, also, often leading up to it, for their sweet aroma is said to help the dead find their way. Of course many altars contain photographs and memorabilia of the dead family members who will come to visit. A final touch is a glass or gourd of fresh water, for the dead will be thirsty after their long journey back.

Día de los Muertos amounts to a joyous reunion of all family members—both living and dead. Death is part of the inevitable flow of life, and in Mexico, on this special day, the truth of this is acknowledged and lived.

Guadalupe, Soledad, and Navidad

The month of December in Oaxaca nearly amounts to a nonstop fiesta that kicks off with celebrations leading up to Mexico's patron day, **Virgen de la Guadalupe** (Dec. 12), after which Oaxacans continue feting their own patron, the **Virgen de la Soledad** (Dec. 16-18). Festivities, which center around the Virgin's basilica (on Independencia, six blocks west of the *zócalo*), include fireworks, dancing, food, and street processions of the faithful, bearing the Virgin's gold-crowned image decked out in her fine silks and satins.

Soon comes the **Fiesta de los Rábanos** (Festival of the Radishes; Dec. 23), when celebrants fill the Oaxaca *zócalo,* admiring amazing displays of plants, flowers, and whimsical figures crafted of giant radishes. Ceremonies and prizes honor the most innovative designs. Food stalls nearby serve traditional delicacies, including *buñuelos* (honey-soaked fried tortillas), plates of which are traditionally thrown into the air before the evening is over.

Oaxacans culminate their pre-Christmas week on **Nochebuena** (Christmas Eve) with candlelit processions from their parishes, accompanied by music, fireworks, and floats. They converge on the *zócalo* in time for a midnight cathedral mass.

Other Festivals

Besides the usual national holidays, a number of other locally important fiestas liven up the Oaxaca calendar. The first day of spring, March 21, kicks off the **Juegos Florales** (Flower Games). Festivities go on for 10 days, including the crowning of a festival queen at the Teatro Alcalá, poetry contests, and performances by renowned artists and the National Symphony.

On the second Monday in October, residents of Santa María del Tule venerate their ancient tree in the **Lunes del Tule** festival. Locals in costume celebrate with rites, folk dances, and feats of horsemanship beneath the boughs of their beloved great cypress.

ARTS EVENTS

Many Oaxaca institutions, such as the **Museo de Arte Contemporaneo de Oaxaca** (Macedonio Alcalá 202, tel. 951/514-1055, www.museomaco.com), the **Teatro Alcalá** (900 Independencia, tel. 951/516-8312 or 951/516-8344), the **Instituto de Artes Gráficos de Oaxaca** (across Macedonio Alcalá, tel. 951/516-6980), and the art-film **Cinema El Pochote** (García Vigil 817, tel.

Catrina, Queen of the Day of the Dead

Catrina Calavera, stylish queen of the Day of the Dead

While Día de los Muertos has its roots in Aztec rituals several thousand years old, and other elements draw on Catholic holidays and ceremonies imported by the Spanish, some of the imagery and activity associated with this most beloved of Mexican holidays is of a newer vintage.

Take Catrina, for example. All those skeletal women with fancy hats and dresses you'll see, either live, in paper mache, or perhaps in a candy version around November 1, are all versions of Catrina, whose origins lie not in pre-Hispanic Mexico but in the 19th century. A famous Mexican illustrator named José Guadalupe Posada created a print of a figure he called La Calavera Catrina (The Elegant Skull). Meant as a parody of an upper-class Mexican woman (striving to be as white-skinned as possible), the figure of Catrina, with her gown and usually impossibly fancy hat, soon took on a life of her own.

Today, the well-costumed female with a skeleton face and a fancy hat has become a ubiquitous presence on Dia de los Muertos. Girls who want to dress up on this holiday often turn themselves into Catrina, with faces painted to look like skulls, big hats, and elaborate gowns. You'll find Catrina comes in all shapes and sizes all over Oaxaca and indeed all over Mexico on November 1.

951/514-1194, films at 6pm and 8pm Tues.-Sat.), sponsor first-rate cultural events, as do the owners of Oaxaca's premier bohemian hipster bar, **Café Central** (Hidalgo 302, tel. 951/514-2042, colectivocentral.com, 9pm-2am Wed.-Sat.), who offer free movies of an independent persuasion on Wednesday evenings.

Local sources of events information include resident Diane Barclay's top-notch website (www.oaxacacalendar.com), the weekly Spanish *El Grito*, events newsletter of the **Oaxaca State Secretary of Culture** (www.cultura.oaxaca.gob.mx), and **Oaxaca state tourist information office** (703 Av. Juárez, west side of El Llano park, www.aoaxaca.com).

NIGHTLIFE

When lacking an official fiesta, you can create your own at a number of nightspots around town.

Some sidewalk cafés around the *zócalo* regularly have live music. Just follow the sound to either café **Terranova** (tel. 951/516-4747) or **El Importador** (southeast *zócalo* corner, tel. 951/514-3200) next door, or the marimba band in front of the café **Del Jardín** (southwest corner, tel. 951/516-2092).

Founded in 1916, **Bar La Farola** (20 de Noviembre 314, corner of Las Casas, tel. 951/516-5352, 11am-2am daily), a block west and a block south of the *zócalo,* claims to be Oaxaca's longest-running cantina. The Farola's dignified old-style-pub ambience attracts a middle-to-upper-class local clientele, some young, some old, who come to relax over food, drinks, and the rhythms of a live Latin-jazz-salsa trio.

One of the most intense in-town nightspots is **Candela** (Murguia 413, corner of Pino Suárez, tel. 951/514-2010, from about 10pm Thurs.-Sat.), which jumps with hot salsa and African-Latin rhythms. Arrive at 10pm for dance lessons; call to confirm.

Very popular among twentysomethings is **Bar La Pasion** (tucked beyond the rear of Restaurant Mayordomo, Macedonio Alcalá 302, tel. 951/514-4363 or 951/516-6113, noon-3am daily), with giant flat-screen TVs, studio lighting, and loud, live music.

La Condesa Coffee Bar (Cinco de Mayo 413, on the corner of Adolfo Gurrion, tel. 951/514-1806) is a high-ceilinged, multi-room hangout—coffee bar by day, drinking bar by night—for Oaxacan and visiting hipsters of all ages. The style is ultra-cool, the music is loud, and the lighting is intense, but if this is your kind of thing this is one good place to do it. Hours are flexible, credit cards are accepted, and there are plenty of excellent *mezcals* on the menu.

El Barracuda (García Vigil 416, no phone listed, late hours) is a hard core rock n' roll bar that opens late and stays open later.

For a taste of a great, single distillery *mezcal*—in several different styles—don't miss a stop at **Mezcaleria Los Amantes** (Allende 107, 4pm-10pm daily, tel. 951/501-0687, losamantes.com), one of Oaxaca City's most interesting little "bars." More like a mini-museum, Los Amantes is the work of mezcalero Horacio Arenas. He's the guy who comes in almost every night and plays acoustic guitar and sings beautiful Mexican songs. You can do a sampling of *blanco, reposado,* and *añejo* for about $8. The tiny room is a work of art, as are the mezcals Arenas cooks up at his distillery. This place is one of a kind! (If you happen to be in New York City, drop by the Casa Mezcal at 86 Orchard Street and get a little taste of Los Amantes without going south of the border.)

Café Central (Hidalgo 302, tel. 951/516-8505, 9pm-2am Wed.-Sat.) is the art-bar project of Oaxacan artist Guillermo Olguín, who shows independent films for free on Wednesdays, offers live music on Thursdays and Fridays ($3), and turns the whole place into a rocking, free-entry dance club on Saturdays.

For a more subdued atmosphere, try the luxury hotels, which host live dance music in their lobby bars, especially on weekends and holidays. Call to confirm programs at **Camino Real** (Cinco de Mayo 300, tel. 951/516-0611, www.caminoreal.com/Oaxaca) and **Hotel Victoria** (Km 545, Blvd. Adolfo Ruiz Cortínez 1306, Carretera Panamericana, tel. 951/515-2633, www.hotelvictoriaoax.com.mx).

Tlaxaparta (Matamoros 206, tel. 951/514-4305) serves as hookah club by day (with a good low priced set lunch) and kicks into gear as a dance club around midnight. It's a lively scene for all ages, visitors and locals alike.

La Cantinita (Macedonio Alcalá 303, tel. 951/516-8961) draws plenty of tourists and a smattering of locals due to its prime location on the Alcalá. The joint is liveliest on weekends, with live music many nights, otherwise a DJ keeps the beat. Throw in free *botanas* (snacks) and bottle service (buy a whole bottle instead of a series of cocktails), and you've got yourself a party.

At **La Divina** (Adolfo Gurion 104, tel. 951/582-0508) local and visiting bands churn out heavy metal and other forms of hard, live rock and roll, drawing young visitors and locals into the club's surrealist interior until the wee hours.

La Tentacion (Matamoros 101, tel. 951/514-9521, $1-3 cover) offers another late night scene: after 10pm the salsa band kicks in and the crowd cuts loose. When the band is not on, the DJ is, mixing Mexican and international pop. People wait in line to get in here.

La Casa de Mezcal (Flores Magón 209, tel. 951/156 4285) has been open since 1935, earning it accolades as one of Oaxaca City's original taverns. Mezcal-lovers take note: this bar specializes in mezcal made from a wild agave called Tobala, which grows only at high altitudes in the shade of oak trees.

If you are looking for gay Oaxacan nightlife, **Bar 502** (Porfirio Díaz 502, no phone) is open weekend nights, and draws a mixed gender clientele who arrive late and dance until dawn.

El Piano y El Sofa (20 de Noviembre #103A, tel. 951/191-3060) is a bar and dance club that offers live jazz and blues rather than rock. The style is vintage chic, but the mood is utterly contemporary.

For great international food with an Italian slant, and live music in one package, try **El Sol y La Luna** (Reforma 502, tel. 951/514-8069), where jazz, salsa, merengue, and all manner of Latin music is played live several nights a week. Call to see who's on the bill.

Sports and Recreation

MOUNTAIN BIKING

For adventurous types, a fantastic way to explore the mountains of Oaxaca is with the guides from **Bicicletas Pedro Martinez Tours** (Aldama 418, tel. 951/514-5935, bicicletgaspedromartinez.com), a mountain biking company with offices located on the southwest side of town a few blocks from the Mercado Juárez. Martinez is a former Mexican Olympic team cyclist so he knows his stuff. Private and group biking and hiking tours can range from half-day trips to multi-day tours encompassing trails all over the state with serious trans-Sierra climbs involved. Food, water, guides, support vehicles (which will haul people up the hard hills if need be), and well-maintained bikes are included. Contact the office or tour the website for details on the company's many interesting and unusual trips.

The shortest trips are half-day or full-day rides in the Valle de Tlacolula or up into Llano Grande or around Monte Albán, or up into the Hierve de Agua region: the full-day trips cost about $100 per person for two people or $90 per person for four including bikes, guide, lunch, water, and transportation to starting points and back to Oaxaca City. For ultra-adventurous souls, the company offers a four-day tour that starts in Oaxaca and ends in Puerto Escondido, with a mix of camping and hotels along the way through the mountains. Bikes, gloves, guides, meals, and transportation back to Oaxaca provided for prices ranging from $400 to $500 per person, depending on the size of the group and the state of the peso. You will see parts of Oaxaca that no tourists ever see, except those on bikes.

HORSEBACK RIDING

There are a number of guest ranchos just outside Oaxaca City that offer horseback riding adventures in the countryside around Oaxaca Valley. One that comes highly recommended is **Rancho Pitaya** in the Tlacolula Valley. Their short version is a half-day trip, for about $70, that includes round-trip transport from their **office in Oaxaca City** (Murguia 403, tel. 951/199-7026 in Oaxaca, tel. 310/929-7099 from the U.S.) and a two-hour ride with an English-speaking guide. Longer versions include full-day and multi-day rides with overnight stays at the rancho or at cabins up in the mountains, at costs up to $525 per person. Everything is discounted for larger parties. This is another off-the-road option for experiencing Oaxaca's ruggedly gorgeous backcountry while avoiding the hordes of high-season tourists.

SWIMMING, TENNIS, AND GOLF

Swimmers can do their laps and laze the afternoon away by the big pool (unheated but usually swimmable) at in-town **Hotel Rivera del Ángel** (Mina 518, tel. 951/516-6666, $10 adults, $5 kids ages 5 and under).

For both tennis (about seven courts) and a nine-hole golf course, go to the relaxed country club-style **Club Brenamiel** (intersection of Hwy. 190 and Calle San Jacinto, tel. 951/512-6822, clubbrenamiel@hotmail.com), about three miles north of the town center, on the left just past the Hotel Villas del Sol. Alternatively, on the other side of town, try the well-equipped (half a dozen tennis courts, two pools, gymnasium) YMCA-like **Deportivo Oaxaca** (Km 6.5, Carretera a El Tule, tel. 951/517-5271, 951/517-5974, or 951/517-7312), off Highway 190 on the way to El Tule, about four miles east of town. *Note:* Although both Club Brenamiel and Deportivo Oaxaca are membership organizations, they do accept day guests for a fee.

You can also take a swim at **Balneario Vista Hermosa** (Hidalgo 18 San Agustín Etla, tel. 951/521-2049), or play a round of golf at **Club de Golf Vista Hermosa** (Carretera a San Agustín Etla, tel. 951/547-1177), in the nearby town of San Agustín Etla, about half an hour north of the city.

For both swimming and tennis, you can also stay at either the **Hotel Victoria** (Km 545, Blvd. Adolfo Ruiz Cortínez 1306, Carretera Panamericana, tel. 951/515-2633, www.hotelvictoriaoax.com.mx) or the **Hotel Misión de los Angeles** (Porfirio Díaz 102, tel. 951/502-0100, www.misiondelosangeles.com).

WALKING

For an invigorating in-town walk, climb the **Cerro del Fortín.** Your reward will be a panoramic city, valley, and mountain view. The key to getting there through the maze of city streets is to head to the **Escalera del Fortín** (staircase), which will lead you conveniently to the instep of the hill. For example, from the northeast *zócalo* corner, walk north along the Macedonio Alcalá mall. After five blocks, in front of the Iglesia de Santo Domingo, turn left onto Allende, continue four blocks to Crespo, and turn right. After three blocks, you'll see the staircase on the left. Continue uphill, past the sprawling Guelaguetza open-air auditorium, to the road (Av. Nicolas Copernicus) heading north to the **Planetario Nundehui** (tel. 951/514-5379, 8am-3pm and 7pm-9pm daily Nov.-May, $1.50 adults, $1 kids, check the events schedule), where you can enjoy the panoramic city and valley view. (Besides daytime movies and star shows, the planetarium is customarily open for evening telescopic viewings of the moon, planets, and stars.) Past the planetarium, you can keep walking along the hilltop for at least another mile. Wear a hat and bring water. The round-trip from the *zócalo* is a minimum of two miles; the hilltop rises only a few hundred feet. Allow at least a couple of hours.

Shopping

The city of Oaxaca is renowned as a handicraft shopper's paradise. Prices are moderate, quality is high, and sources—in both large traditional markets and many dozens of private stores and galleries—are manifold. In the city, however, vendors do not ordinarily make the merchandise they sell. They buy wholesale from family shops in town, the surrounding valley, and remote localities all over the state of Oaxaca and Mexico in general. If your time is severely limited, it's best to buy from the good in-town sources, many of which are recommended here.

TRADITIONAL MARKETS

The original town market, **Mercado Juárez,** covers the entire square block just one block south and one block west of the *zócalo.* Many dozens of stalls offer everything; cotton and wool items—such as dresses, *huipiles,* woven blankets, and serapes—are among the best buys. Despite the overwhelming festoons of merchandise, bargains are there for those willing to search them out.

Before diving into Juárez market's cavernous interior, first orient yourself by looking over the lineup of stalls on the market's west side, along the block of 20 de Noviembre, between Las Casas and Trujano. Here, you'll be able to select from a reasonably priced representative assortment—*alebrijes* (fanciful wooden animals), black and green pottery, cutlery, filigree jewelry, *huipiles,* leather goods, pewter, tinware—of much that Oaxaca offers.

If organic food and produce suits your style, visit the modest **Pochote Market** (411 Rayon, corner of Xicotencatl, most shops 9am-4pm daily), four blocks east and two blocks south of the *zócalo's* southeast corner. A sprinkling of vendors from all over the Valley of Oaxaca offer fruit, vegetables, homemade mezcal, honey, delicious hot tecate (tay-KAH-tay) chocolate-flavored drink, and lots of fresh food cooked on the spot.

After your Juárez market tour, walk along Aldama, a block west, to J. P. Garcia, then left, one and a half blocks south, to between Mina and Zaragoza, for a look inside the **Mercado de Artesanías** (handicrafts market). Here, you'll find a ton of textiles—fetching *huipiles* and *camisas* (shirts), flowery *blusas* (blouses), fine wool *tapetes* (carpets), colorful *alfarería* (pottery), whimsical *alebrijes,* festive handmade masks, and much more.

PRIVATE HANDICRAFTS SHOPS

Although pricier, the private shops generally offer the choicest merchandise. Here you can select from the very best: *huipiles* from San Pedro de Amusgos and Yalalag; richly embroidered "wedding" dresses from San Antonino Castillo Velasco; rugs and hangings from Teotitlán del Valle and Santa Ana del Valle; pottery (black from San Bartolo Coyotepec and green from Atzompa); carved *alebrijes* from Arrazola; whimsical figurines by the Aguilar sisters of Ocotlán; mezcal from Tlacolula; and masks from Huazolotitlán.

Most of the best individual shops lie scattered along three streets—Cinco de Mayo, Macedonio Alcalá, and García Vigil, which run uphill, north of the *zócalo.*

★ MARO

Somewhere along your handicrafts route, you must take a serious look around **MARO, Mujeres Artesanías de las Regiones de Oaxaca** (Craftswomen of the Regions of Oaxaca; 204 Cinco de Mayo, tel./fax 951/516-0670, 9am-7:30pm daily). From behind Oaxaca Cathedral, walk uphill, along Macedonio Alcalá, first passing Independencia; one block farther, at Morelos, turn right, continue a block and turn left on Cinco de Mayo, and walk half a block uphill to MARO, on the right.

Here, a remarkable all-Oaxaca grassroots movement of women artisans sell their goods and demonstrate their manufacturing techniques. The artisans are native Mexicans from all parts of Oaxaca, and their offerings reflect their unique effort. The shelves of several rooms are filled with hosts of gorgeous handicrafts: wooden masks, toys, carvings; cotton *traje* (native clothing), such as *huipiles, pozahuancos,* and *quechquémitles;* wool serapes, rugs, and hangings; woven palm hats, mats, and baskets; fine steel knives, swords, and machetes; tinplate mirrors, candlesticks, and ornaments; and leather saddles, briefcases, wallets, and belts. Don't miss it. Better still, do a major part of your Oaxaca shopping at this store.

Other Private Shops

South of the *zócalo,* head up J. P. Garcia and visit the unique private store **El Arte Oaxaqueño** (Mina 317, corner of J. P. Garcia, tel. 951/516-1581, 10am-8pm Mon.-Sat., 10am-5pm Sun.). The diverse, carefully selected offerings run from lovely wool weavings and bright one-of-a-kind pottery to fetching wooden toys and precious metal Christmas ornaments. Each piece comes with a detailed explanation of its history and a description of the craftsperson that made it.

Continue north on Macedonio Alcalá for a block and step into **La Mano Mágico** (Macedonio Alcalá 203, on the west side, just below corner of Murguia, tel./fax 951/516-4275, 10:30am-3pm and 4pm-8pm Mon.-Sat.). The shop offers both a colorful exposition of crafts from all over Mexico and a patio workshop where artisans work, dyeing wool and weaving examples of the lovely, museum-quality rugs and serapes that adorn the walls.

Take a one-block detour west along Matamoros to **Casa de Artesaniás** (Matamoros 105, corner of García Vigil, tel. 951/516-5062, 9am-9pm Mon.-Sat., 10am-6pm Sun.). Here, a cooperative of about six dozen Oaxaca artisan families offers a wide handicrafts selection, including rainbows of fantastic *alebrijes*, from Tilcajete and Arrazola, a treasury of glistening black pottery from Coyotepec, and preciously embroidered dresses from San Antonio Castillo Velasco.

Return and continue uphill on Macedonio Alcalá, a block farther north, to the Plaza Alcalá complex (southwest corner of M. Bravo), which has both an outstanding courtyard restaurant, Hostería Alcalá, and some good shops. Best among them is an exceptional bookstore, **Librería Amate** (307 Macedonio Alcalá, tel. 951/516-6960 or 951/516-7181, amatebooks@prodigy.net.mx, 10:30am-7:30pm Mon.-Sat., 2pm-7pm Sun.). Personable owner Henry Wangeman stocks an expertly selected library of English-language books about Mexico, including archaeology, cookbooks, ethnography, guides, history, literature, maps, postcards, and much more.

If you're interested in fine weavings, step directly across Macedonio Alcalá at the corner of Gurrion to **Tapetes de Teotitlán** (Macedonio Alcalá, tel. 951/516-1675, 11am-7:30pm Mon.-Sat., 1pm-7pm Sun.), the shop of the Martínez family from the famous Teotitlán del Valle weaving village. Here, you're looking at the real thing: fine, mostly traditional designs, made of all-natural dyes.

Half a block farther uphill, be sure to look inside jewelry store **Oro de Monte Albán** (Macedonio Alcalá 403, tel. 951/514-3813, 10am-8pm Mon.-Sat., noon-8pm Sun.), across from the Iglesia de Santo Domingo. This extraordinary family-run enterprise carries on Oaxaca's venerable goldsmithing tradition as the sole licensed manufacturer of replicas from the renowned treasure of Monte Albán Tomb 7. Besides the luscious, museum-quality reproductions, Oro de Monte Albán offers a fine assortment of in-house silver and gold earrings, charm bracelets, necklaces, brooches, and much more. There are now three of these **Oro de Monte Albán** shops within a block of each other along the Alcalá; one does jewelry only, the others offer jewelry plus a wide selection of T-shirts and sweatshirts with often dazzling Oaxacan-inspired imagery printed on them.

CLOTHING AND TEXTILES

While you're on Macedonio Alcalá, be sure to peruse the colorful outdoor displays of for-sale local paintings and native-style women's *blusas, enredos, vestidos* (blouses, skirts, dresses), and *huipiles* that decorate **Plaza Labastida,** just south, across Abasolo, from the Santo Domingo church.

And if you want to know what's up with contemporary Oaxacan textile and clothing design, there are at least half a dozen retail stores within a few blocks, most run by their owner/designers, offering collections of one-of-a-kind, tradition-grounded clothes and textiles. These stores are for the most part not inexpensive, but you might find something—one thing—that is just perfect, an inspired interpretation of vintage Oaxaca with style enough for New York or Paris. The following is a sample: there are many others in the neighborhood worth visiting.

Huizache (Murguia 101 at Alcalá, tel. 951/501-1282, 10am-8pm daily) is a large, lovely store offering work from a collective of about 100 Oaxacan artisans, clothing designers, and craftspeople from all over the country. It's well worth a visit to check out the beautiful clothes as well as the pottery. A loom and a spinning wheel on site allow shoppers an opportunity to see how the fabric is made.

Fabiola Calvo Arte Textil (Cinco de Mayo 101, Macedonio Alcalá 501, tel. 951/516-0445, 10am-6pm) does the new-old mix with panache. The designs are ultra-chic and sexy, but the patterns of the textiles are traditional.

At **Reallstmo** (Cinco de Mayo 315-A, Murguia 101-5, tel. 951/515-1174 or 951/205-4516) find beautifully-rendered modern clothing, shoes, handbags, and other accessories done in the bright, colorful fabrics of Tehuantepec (in the Isthmus, hence the name). High-topped lace-up tennies, done Tehuantepec style? Why not? They look great.

Designer Odilon Merino Morales of **Arte Amuzgo** (Cinco de Mayo 217-B, tel. 951/516-9104 or 951/210-4089) works with the traditional textiles of the Amuzco people, who occupy a small piece of territory on the Oaxaca-Guerrero border. The patterns are geometrically-inspired and quietly colorful; she has reinterpreted the traditional in a fresh, modern way.

FINE ART GALLERIES

The tourist boom has stimulated a Oaxaca fine-arts revival. Several downtown galleries bloom with the sculpture and paintings of masters, such as Rufino Tamayo, Rudolfo Morales, Francisco Toledo, and a host of up-and-coming local artists. Besides **La Mano Mágico** (Macedonio Alcalá 203, on the west side, just below corner of Murguia, tel./fax 951/516-4275, 10:30am-3pm and 4pm-8pm Mon.-Sat.), one of the private handicrafts shops, a number of galleries stand out. Foremost among them is **Arte de Oaxaca** (Murguia 105, between Macedonio Alcalá and Cinco de Mayo, tel. 951/514-0910, www.artedeoaxaca.com, 11am-3pm and 5pm-8pm Mon.-Fri., 11am-6pm Sat.), the gallery of the Rudolfo Morales Foundation.

Also outstanding is **Galería Quetzalli** (Constitución 104, between Reforma and Cinco de Mayo, tel. 951/514-2606, fax 951/514-0735, www.galeriaquetzalli.com, 10am-2pm and 5pm-8pm Mon.-Sat.), local outlet for celebrated artist Francisco Toledo. It's located opposite the south flank of Iglesia de Santo Domingo.

There are several other galleries in the neighborhood of Quetzalli; they primarily exhibit contemporary art by Oaxacan painters, sculptors, and artists in other media. For the most part these galleries open at 10am and close at 8pm daily; some take a mid-day break. In our most recent visit we found interesting contemporary work at all of the following galleries: **Galería 910 Arte Contemporaneo** (Alcalá 305 interior 3 y 4—upstairs, tel. 951/516-9862); **Galería Linda Fernandez** (Gurríon 104-1, tel. 951/171-6205); **Didier Mayés** (Cinco de Mayo 409-B, tel. 951/501-2352, didier-mayes.com). We found some great work in the gallery that is next door to and operated by the owners of the **Decó Enmarcados art supply store** (Reforma 407-A, tel. 951/205-0597) as well. If you are in the neighborhood, you'll find other galleries that might have something you can take home. Oaxaca is currently a hotbed of contemporary art. There is fine work in styles ranging from abstract to surreal to expressionist and everything in between, and, for the most part, the work is not at all overpriced.

CURIOSITY SHOPS

A few blocks away from the fine arts galleries is the longtime coin, antique bric-a-brac, and art store **Monedas y Antiguidades** (Coins and Antiques; Abasolo 107, between the upper end of Cinco de Mayo and Reforma, tel. 951/516-3935, 11am-3pm and 6pm-9pm Mon.-Sat.). Browsers enjoy a potpourri of art, from kitsch to fine, plus a for-sale museum of dusty curios, from old silver coins and pioneer clothes irons to revolutionary photos and Porfirian-era tubas.

CUTLERY AND METALWORK SHOPS

Oaxaca is well known for its fine metal crafts. A few families produce nearly everything. A couple of the families sell their wares from their own shops. While in Mercado Juárez, stop by stall number 5 to see the fine swords, knives, and scissors of **Miguel Martínez** and family (Mercado Juárez, tel. 951/514-4868, 9am-9pm Mon.-Sat., 9am-6pm Sun.). Walk a few blocks west and south to see an even wider selection, plus artisans at work, at **Guillermo Aragon**'s street-front shop (J. P. Garcia 503, tel. 951/516-2658, 10:30am-3pm and 4pm-8pm Mon.-Sat.).

SPORTING GOODS AND CLOTHES

A modest sporting goods and clothing selection (no tennis rackets at this writing, however) is available at **Deportes Ziga** (southwest corner of Macedonio Alcalá and Matamoros, next to La Mano Mágico handicrafts shop, tel. 951/514-1654, 9am-3pm and 4pm-9pm Mon.-Sat., 11am-2pm Sun.). There is at least one **Walmart** on Oaxaca's outskirts these days. You'll pass it coming into town from the airport. No doubt they stock plenty of underpriced sporting goods and clothes.

Accommodations

Oaxaca offers a wide range of good lodgings. Air-conditioning is not particularly necessary in temperate Oaxaca, although hot-water showers (furnished by all lodgings listed here, though the budget hotels and hostels often have warm rather than hot water, with sketchy water pressure) feel especially comfy during cool winter mornings and evenings. Many of the less expensive hotels, which generally do not accept credit cards, are within easy walking distance of the colorful, traffic-free *zócalo*. Every hotel we have listed offers free Wi-Fi: most often, you will get it, however slow, in your room, but in some cases you might have to go to a lobby area.

During holidays and festivals (pre-Easter week, July, August, late October-early November, December 15-January 6), most Oaxaca hotels and bed-and-breakfasts raise their prices 10-50 percent above the rates listed here. Several of the following lodgings and many more not listed here are advertised on **websites,** such as www.hotelesdeoaxaca.com for **hotels,** www.oaxacabedandbreakfast.org for **bed-and-breakfasts,** and www.vrbo.com (**Vacation Rentals by owner**) for long-term house and apartment rentals.

All accommodations listed in this section are positive recommendations, grouped by location in relation to the *zócalo,* and listed, within each location group, in ascending order of double-occupancy price. Almost all of the hotels listed have tour offices or people on staff who can help you plan tours to Oaxaca Valley destinations.

The number of Oaxaca bed-and-breakfast-style lodgings has increased in response to the influx of North American visitors. From only a scant few a generation ago, Oaxaca has blossomed with perhaps two dozen attractive bed-and-breakfasts located mostly on the north side, uphill from the town center. As a group, they are not particularly economical, since they are a North American transplant that appeals to foreign visitors who are accustomed to paying somewhat elevated prices. The recommendations that follow present a sampling of several of the most solid, long-standing Oaxaca bed-and-breakfasts. For even more choices, check out the good website, www.oaxacabedandbreakfast.org.

NEAR THE ZÓCALO
Under $50

For economy and value, consider **Hotel El Chapulin** (Aldama 317, tel. 951/516-1646, hotelchapulin@hotmail.com, $16 s, $20 d, $24 t), one of Oaxaca's fine budget lodgings. The welcoming owners carefully tend to the eight rooms, which are tucked away from street traffic noise. The result: a restful, clean, two-story retreat climaxed by an airy rooftop patio with a superb view of town, and the towering Monte Albán ridge above the southern horizon as the backdrop. All of this plus private shower-bath, Wi-Fi, and inviting lobby-sitting room is available for less than $25.

Head northeast a few blocks east of the zócalo's northeast corner to the busy, budget traveler-favorite, the 39-room **Posada del Virrey** (1001 Morelos, tel. 951/516-5555, fax 951/516-2193, $35 s or d in one bed, $45 d in two beds, $50 t). Only four blocks (five minutes) east of the zócalo, the authentically colonial Posada del Virrey offers two floors of rooms surrounding a spacious inner restaurant patio. The rooms are comfortably furnished, including one, two, or three double beds. Rooms come with cable TV, phone, fan, and parking (9pm-9am); MasterCards are accepted.

Even closer in, just half a block west of the zócalo's southwest corner, is the popular **Hotel Las Rosas** (Trujano 112, tel./fax 951/514-2217, $41 s, $47 d, $53 t). Climb a flight of stairs to the small lobby, relatively tranquil by virtue of its 2nd-floor location. Beyond that, a double tier of rooms surrounds a homey inner patio. Adjacent to the lobby is a cheery sitting room with a tropical aquarium and a TV, usually kept at subdued volume. In the rear, guests enjoy an airy terrace for reading and relaxing. The rooms themselves, although plainly furnished, are clean and tiled. Prices are very reasonable for such a well-located hotel. Discounts are negotiable for a one-week stay. No credit cards, parking, or wheelchair access, however.

A block west of the zócalo's southwest corner, find the **Hotel Santa Rosa** (Trujano 201, tel. 951/514-6714 or 951/514-6715, fax 951/514-6715, hostalsantarosa@hotmail.com, $40 s, $48 d). The streetside lobby leads past an airy restaurant to the rooms, recessed along a meandering inner passageway and courtyard. Inside, the rooms are comfortably furnished and decorated in pastels. Rates continue to be reasonable except during festivals and holidays, when they might rise as much as 40 percent. Hotel Santa Rosa offers TV, phones, parking, limited wheelchair access, and an in-house travel-tour agency, but credit cards are not accepted.

$50-100

Just a block south of the zócalo's southwest corner, the ★ **Hotel Trebol** (Flores Magón 201, tel./fax 951/516-1256, www.oaxaca-mio.com/trebol.htm, $50 s or d in one bed, $70 d in two beds, $80 t) remains an enduring, brightly-painted jewel among Oaxaca's moderately priced hotels. Guests can choose from about 40 rooms, artfully sprinkled in three stories around an airy, plant-decorated inner patio. The rooms are comfortably furnished with rustic tile, hand-hewn wooden furniture, table lamps, color-coordinated bedspreads, and shower-baths. Rooms include fans, telephone, cable TV, and Wi-Fi; there's also a travel agent and a good restaurant in the hotel.

Ideally situated just east of the zócalo's northeast corner, the best-buy colonial-era **Hotel Real de Antequera** (Hidalgo 807, tel. 951/516-4635, fax 951/516-7511, www.oaxaca-mio.com/real.htm, $45 s, $55 d, $65 t) offers plenty for reasonable rates. The 29 comfortable rooms, in two stories around an inviting old world-style restaurant-patio, include breakfast, bath, fans, cable TV, Internet in most rooms, phones, and parking (8:30pm-8:30am), and credit cards are accepted.

Just a few doors south of the zócalo's southeast corner, consider the popular 1980s-mod **Hotel Gala** (Bustamante 103, tel. 951/514-2251 or 951/514-1305, fax 951/516-3660, Mex. toll-free 800/712-7316, www.gala.com.mx, $60 s, $68 d, $76 t, $86 junior suite). Guests enjoy comfortable, modern, deluxe accommodations at relatively moderate prices right in the middle of the *zócalo* action. The 36 rooms, although tastefully decorated and carpeted, are smallish. Get one of the quieter ones away from the street. Rooms include private shower-baths, phones, TVs, and fans; conveniently, the downstairs has a restaurant, and there is parking (10pm-8am); credit cards are accepted.

Return just two blocks west of the *zócalo*'s northwest corner to the class-act ★ **Parador San Miguel** (Independencia 503, tel./fax 951/514-9331, www.paradorsanmigueloaxaca.com, $100 s or d, $110 t). Here, little seems to have been spared in transforming a colonial-era mansion into a lovely hotel. Inside, a plethora of old-world details—leafy, tranquil inner patio; sunny upstairs corridors; brilliant stained glass-decorated staircase; scrolled wrought-iron railings; handsome, hand-carved wooden doors—are bound to please lovers of traditional refinement. A correspondingly elegant restaurant, the Andariega, completes the picture. The 19 rooms and four suites are no less than you'd expect, attractively furnished with custom-woven bedspreads and curtains, handcrafted bamboo and leather furniture, elegantly tiled shower-baths, and a choice of king, single, or double beds. Add about 50 percent to price during festivals and holidays. All rooms come with air-conditioning, cable TV, phones, and wireless Internet. Credit cards are accepted.

NORTH AND EAST OF THE *ZÓCALO*
Under $50

With its rustic, stone-floored lobby and bustling atmosphere, the **Hotel Posada La Casa De La Tia** (Cinco de Mayo 108, tel. 951/514-1963, posadalacasadelatia.com, $30 s, $35 d, $40 t) is a welcoming low-budget option two blocks northeast of the *zócalo*. The clean, well-lit, and comfortable rooms are finished with traditional textile bedspreads, and come relatively cheap considering the fine location. Amenities include Wi-Fi, security lockers, a computer for guest use, cable TV, tour desk, auto rental service, and a restaurant/bar on the premises.

Nearby stands another well-located, moderately-priced choice, the **Hotel Villa de León** (Reforma 405, tel. 951/516-1958 or 951/516-1977, www.hotelesdeoaxaca.com/hotelvilladeleon.html, $30 s, $40 d, $50 t), adjoining the back side of the Iglesia de Santa Domingo grounds. Past the reception and inner-courtyard restaurant, about half of the 20 rooms encircle an upstairs balcony; the remainder are tucked in the rear, fortunately removed from street and restaurant noise. All rooms have tile floors, handmade wooden furniture, and private shower-baths. Credit cards are accepted. Reserve a room away from the heavily trafficked street.

One of the most popular modestly-priced options, ★ **Casa Arnel** (Aldama 404, Colonia Jalatlaco, tel./fax 951/515-2856, www.casaarnel.com.mx, $45 s, $50 d, $55 t) is also farthest north from the *zócalo*. Casa Arnel stands at the edge of downtown, so removed from the urban bustle that it feels as if it's embedded in another era. In front of Casa Arnel, the streets are cobbled with stone, and across from it stands the ancient church, San Matias Jalatlaco, beside its shady neighborhood plaza. The neighborhood is perking up, with a couple of other new hotels and restaurants, and is also home to Toscana, one of Oaxaca's Italian dining gems. Casa Arnel is a family home that grew into a hotel, with about 20 attractively-furnished rooms with baths, around a jungly garden blooming with birdcalls and flowers. Additional amenities include a broad roof deck with umbrellas, tables, and chairs for sunning and relaxing, a couple of big tables on the patio for communal breakfasting, and on-site tour planning.

$50-100

Behind (east of) the Iglesia de Santo Domingo block, find **La Casa de Rosita** (Reforma 410, tel. 951/516-1982 or 951/514-9815, www.lacasa-de-rosita.com, $60/night, $400/week), formerly La Casa de los Abuelos (House of the Grandparents). This charmingly quirky colonial-era complex is the life project of personable owner-builder Luis Arroyo Nuñez, who inherited it from his *abuelos* (grandparents). This former priests' residence for Iglesia de Santo Domingo was confiscated by the government after the *cristero* revolt of the late 1920s. Luis's six completely renovated apartments, built around two quiet inner patios, are replete with unique details, such as exposed original brick walls, old family photos, bric-a-brac, and sturdy wooden staircases leading up to bedroom lofts. Rentals include invitingly furnished living-dining rooms, kitchenettes, queen-size beds, and shower-baths. Asking rates are negotiable by the month; apartments come with fans, TV, purified bottled water, and Wi-Fi.

In the Santo Domingo neighborhood, discerning travelers should consider the low-key but inviting **Hotel Maela** (Constitución 206, tel./fax 951/516-6022, www.hotelesdeoaxaca.com/maela.htm, $41 s, $51 d, $61 t, suites for four $70), one block east of the Iglesia de Santo Domingo compound. Inside, just past reception, the ceilings are gracefully high, and the 23 rooms and three suites, in two stories, are spacious, with private shower-baths and attractive handmade wood dressers, beds, and end tables. Rooms come with fans or air-conditioning, TV, Wi-Fi, and parking.

On the northwest side, about three blocks west of the Iglesia de Santo Domingo, is the very inviting ★ **Hotel Las Golondrinas** (Tinoco y Palacios 411, tel. 951/514-3298, hotellasgolondrinas.com.mx, $50 s, $55 d, $60 t). Rooms surround an intimate garden, lovingly decorated with festoons of hothouse verdure. Leafy bananas, bright bougainvillea, and platoons of potted plants line pathways that meander past a fountain patio in one corner and lead to an upstairs panoramic vista sundeck in the other. The care also shows in the rooms, which, although smallish, are immaculate and adorned with pastel earth-toned curtains and bedspreads, and natural wood furniture. Guests additionally enjoy use of laundry facilities, a TV room, Wi-Fi, a shelf of paperback books, and a breakfast café (8am-10am) in the garden. In addition to the 27 regular rooms, two honeymoon suites rent for about $60 each.

Right across the street from Las Golondrinas you'll find ★ **Hotel Casa del Sotano** (Tinoco y Palacios 414, tel. 951/516-2494, hoteldelsotano.com, $57-77 s, $69-88 d, $77-97 t), another beautifully put-together small hotel in our medium price range. All 21

a garden patio at Hotel Las Golondrinas

rooms and two suites are finished and furnished in the rich mix of traditional and contemporary style that defines Oaxaca today. The higher rates are for the upper-floor rooms, which have better views of the city. Down below, however, the rooms encircle a lovely patio with plantings and an elegant and soothing water feature. An on-premises café serves breakfast and lunch, remaining open into the afternoon and evening, seasonally. The café specializes in chocolate and mezcal, two Oaxacan favorites. The rooftop deck puts the city on display. Rooms have phones, fans, cable TV, safes, and hair dryers; the hotel will organize tours. Wi-Fi is available in the lobby only.

Several blocks north of Iglesia de Santo Domingo stands the **Hotel Casona de Llano** (Av. Juárez 701, tel. 951/514-7719 or 951/514-7703, fax 951/516-2219, www.hotelcasonadellano.com, $60 s, $70 d, $80 t). This hotel is a favorite of visitors who enjoy the shady, untouristed ambience of Oaxaca's big Sunday park, officially called Parque Paseo Juárez, but popularly referred to as El Llano (YAH-noh, Plain or Flat Place). The 28 rooms include fans, TV, and phones. Parking is available and credit cards are accepted.

On the other side and a block south of El Llano, step into ★ **Hotel Casa Vertíz** (Reforma 404, tel. 951/516-2525, www.hotelvertiz.com.mx, $100 s, $110 d, $140 t), one of the most inviting small hotels in Oaxaca. Here you find a masterfully rebuilt former colonial house with air, light, and space that encourages lingering. Inside the entrance, guests enjoy a refined, airy patio restaurant and a tropical rear garden. All 14 rooms are tucked away from the busy street. Upstairs, rooms open onto a terrace. Accommodations are luxuriously appointed with designer-rustic tile floors, earth-toned bedspreads and curtains, deluxe tiled baths (four rooms have tubs), and queen-size beds. Rentals include cable TV, phone, Wi-Fi, air-conditioning, and parking; credit cards are accepted.

Just south of El Llano park, ★ **Hotel and Studios Las Mariposas** (Pino Suárez 517, tel. 951/515-5854, from U.S./Can. direct tel. 619/793-5121, www.lasmariposas.com.mx, $45 s, $50 d, rate includes breakfast) is strongly recommended as either a bed-and-breakfast, hotel, or apartment rental. Welcoming and knowledgeable owner Teresa Dávila offers 13 rooms (with baths, but no kitchenettes) in her restored 19th-century family house. She also rents five comfortable studio kitchenette suites with private baths

the lively exterior of the Hotel Casa del Sotano

($45 s, $50 d without breakfast). Besides the happy customers, pluses include Wi-Fi, coffee, TV, and use of credit cards (Visa only) for stays of a week or more; kids under 12 are not welcome.

For another worthy, moderately-priced option, check out the **Casa los Arquitos** (Rufino Tamayo 816, tel. 951/132-7951, www.casalosarquitos.com, $65-130), where a welcoming Mexican couple have converted their modest home into an inviting small bed-and-breakfast tucked into the heart of the charming north-end Los Arquitos neighborhood. Their five immaculate rooms with bath, simply but attractively decorated, offer a choice of either one single bed, two single beds, or one king-size bed with full kitchenette, including refrigerator, stove, microwave oven, dishes, and utensils, and a private patio to boot. Amenities include Wi-Fi and a generous continental breakfast with choice of savory organic coffee, hot chocolate, or tea, and breads, yogurt, granola, and fresh seasonal fruit.

Much closer in, just two blocks behind Iglesia de Santo Domingo, you'll find **Casa de las Bugambilias** (Reforma 402, tel./fax 951/516-1165, U.S./Can. toll-free 866/829-6778, www.lasbugambilias.com, $65-95 s, $75-105 d), with seven rooms and one suite, artfully tucked behind its good street-front restaurant. Several rooms open onto a lovely rear garden. Rules include a minimum three-night stay, $50 cancellation fee, children over 12 only, no pets, and no smoking. Amenities include private bath, breakfast, Wi-Fi, a *temazcal* hot room (at extra cost); credit cards are accepted, but parking is not included. The 21 members of the Cabrera-Arroyo family operate this and two other B&Bs nearby; you'll find all three—the others are El Secreto and Casa de los Milagros—elegant and inviting.

Another promising bed-and-breakfast in the same north-side neighborhood (but a few blocks west of El Llano park) is ★ **Bed-and-Breakfast Oaxaca Ollin** (oh-YEEN; Quintana Roo 213, tel. 951/514-9126, U.S./Can. tel. 619/787-5141, www.oaxacaollin.com, $85-135), the project of guide Judith Reyes López and her husband Jon McKinley. Judith and Jon offer 11 comfortable double rooms in their large house, located on a quiet side street a block north and a block east of the Centro Cultural de Santo Domingo. Rooms are comfortably appointed with natural wood furniture, reading lamps, and lovely Talavera-tile bathrooms. Extras abound, such as a swimming pool (not heated, however) and patio, living room, library, reading room, Wi-Fi and local phone calls, and much more. Prices include a hearty Oaxaqueño breakfast.

Back on the northeast side, from Casa de las Bugambilias, go east two blocks and turn north a block to the bed-and-breakfast gem **Casa de Mis Recuerdos** (House of My Memories, Pino Suárez 508, tel. 951/515-8483 or 951/515-5645, www.misrecuerdos.net, U.S. toll-free 877/234-4706, $60-80 s, $95-105 d). Enter the front gate and continue through a bougainvillea-festooned garden to the home of the Valenciana family, which has been accommodating students and foreign visitors for a generation. The rented rooms occupy rear and front sections. The four front rooms, immaculate, spacious, and lovingly decorated with folk art and furnished with handmade wooden furniture, have two bathrooms between them. They are closer to the busy streetfront than the five similarly furnished rear rooms, which, although they have private baths, are smaller.

Over $100

For genuine urbane class, try Oaxaca's most distinguished downtown hotel, the ★ **Camino Real** (Cinco de Mayo 300, tel. 951/516-0611, toll-free U.S./Can. tel. 800/722-6466, fax 951/516-0732, www.caminoreal.com/Oaxaca, $300 d), which occupies the lovingly restored former convent of Santa Catalina, four blocks north and one block east of the *zócalo*. Flowery, secluded courtyards, massive arched portals, soaring beamed ceilings, a big blue pool, and impeccable bar and restaurant service combine to create a refined but relaxed old-world atmosphere. Rooms are large, luxurious, and invitingly decorated with antiques and folk crafts and furnished with a plethora of modern conveniences. The hotel entertains guests and the paying public (about $35 pp) with a weekly class-act, in-house buffet and folkloric dance performance. Rooms have phones and cable TV, but parking is not included; credit cards are accepted.

A more modern take on Oaxacan tradition can be found at the ★ **Hotel Azul** (Abasolo 313, tel. 951/501-0016, hotelazuloaxaca.com, $178-540), where 21 colorful and inviting contemporary rooms and suites surround a stone and cactus patio with a fountain designed by Oaxacan artist Francisco Toledo. Standard rooms with king or two twin beds come with air-conditioning, Wi-Fi, LCD TV, minibar, hair dryer, designer bath products, and telephone. The five suites are designed by different Oaxacan artists; each is unique and wonderful. The in-house restaurant features cuisine from Oaxaca's eight regions, with an emphasis on seafood; the rooftop bar offers inspired views of the heart of the city.

Hotel Misión de Los Angeles (Porfirio Díaz 102, tel. 951/502-0100, fax 951/502-0111, www.oaxaca-mio.com/misiondelosangeles.htm, $140 d, junior suites $155) rambles like a hacienda through a spreading oak- and acacia-decorated garden-park two blocks uphill from Calzada Niños Héroes (Hwy. 190), about a mile uphill, north, of the city center. After a rough few days on the sightseeing circuit, this is an ideal place to kick back beside the big pool or enjoy a set or two of tennis. The 162 rooms and suites are spacious and comfortable, decorated in earth tones and pastels. Many but not all have big garden-view windows or balconies. Additional amenities include phones, air-conditioning, parking, and a restaurant; credit cards are accepted.

The **Hotel Victoria** (Km 545, Blvd. Adolfo Ruiz Cortínez 1306, Carretera Panamericana, tel. 951/5020850, www.hotelvictoriaoax.com.mx, rooms $125, villas $150, junior suites $240) spreads over a lush hillside garden of panoramic vistas and luxurious resort ambience. The 1960s-modern lobby extends from an upstairs bar, downhill past a terrace restaurant, to a flame tree and jacaranda-decorated pool patio. Rooms come in three grades, all comfortably deluxe, that vary by size and location. The smallest are the rooms in the original hotel building; somewhat larger are the villas downstairs around the pool; and most spacious are the junior suites, in the newer wing detached from the lobby building. The 150 rooms come with cable TV, phones, air-conditioning, Wi-Fi, tennis courts, live music seasonally, handicrafts shop, parking, and wheelchair access; credit cards are accepted.

Cooler, breezier San Felipe village, in the foothills north of Oaxaca town, is home to a number of restful luxury lodgings. Choicest among them, ★ **Hacienda Los Laureles** (Hidalgo 21, San Felipe del Agua, tel. 951/501-5300, www.hotelhaciendaloslaureles.com, or agent Mexico Boutique Hotels toll-free U.S./Can. tel. 800/728-9098, www.mexicoboutiquehotels.com, deluxe rooms $300 s or d, superior deluxe $330 s or d) is the labor of love of personable German expatriate owner-managers Ligia and Peter Kaiser. During the late 1990s they rebuilt a venerable hacienda, tenaciously preserving its rustic old-world essence while installing the best of the new. Now, Hacienda Los Laureles's centerpiece is its lush interior garden of grand tropical trees and climbing vines that, at night, is transformed by shadowed lighting and the serenades of crickets and tree frogs into an enchanted forest. The Hacienda's 25 rooms are decorated in elegant simplicity, with high ceilings, handsome tile floors, and hand-hewn mahogany furniture. Bathrooms are likewise luxurious and comfortable. Suites for 3-6 or more people are also available. All come with air-conditioning, cable TV, pool with whirlpool tub, and breakfast at their excellent terrace restaurant. A *temazcal* ceremonial hot room and a menu of spa services are also available at an extra cost.

Elegant **Hotel Casa Oaxaca** (García Vigil 407, tel. 951/514-4173, www.casa-oaxaca.com, $180 s or $242-263 d for the four smallest, yet spacious units, $330 s or d for a larger suite,

$260-407 for a two-story apartment above the rear courtyard) is straight uphill four blocks and a world apart from the *zócalo*. Its sky-blue colonial facade reveals nothing of its singularly unique interior. The lobby, which appears more like an art museum foyer than a lodging entrance, provides the first clue. Past that, you enter a spacious, plant-decorated courtyard, with the wall plaster artfully removed here and there to reveal the brick underlay. Continue to a rear courtyard, which centers on a blue designer pool and a *temazcal*. All six rooms, which border the courtyards, are luxuriously austere and uniquely appointed with antiques, crafts, and contemporary wall art. Rates include gourmet continental breakfast, Wi-Fi, and parking; credit cards are accepted. *Temazcal* treatments, complete with native healer, run about $50 per person.

Apartments

About five blocks north of the *zócalo*, right in front of Iglesia de Santo Domingo, is **Departmentos del Fraile** (Macedonio Alcalá 501, tel./fax 951/516-4310, humbertobenitezc@yahoo.com, $550/month). Family owner-managers offer four compact, modern, and historic (former Santo Domingo priests') apartments, hidden behind a street-front wall and tucked within a quiet, leafy inner courtyard. The renovated units have one bedroom, a bathroom, and a kitchenette. Rentals are monthly only.

SOUTH AND WEST OF THE ZÓCALO
$50-100

Only a few bed-and-breakfast lodgings dot the south and west sides of town. Here are two gems.

Start several blocks southeast of the *zócalo* with **Posada de Chencho** (4ta Privada de la Noria 115, tel./fax 951/514-0043, www.mex-online.com/chencho.htm, $37 s, $49 d, 54 t, without breakfast, add about $6 with breakfast). Chencho is in his 90s and retired now, but his son Antonio carries on the welcoming tradition. Twenty-two immaculate rooms in two stories surround an inviting garden patio. The rooms themselves are comfortably and thoughtfully decorated, with Western-standard baths. Downstairs, guests enjoy a dining room and a big sitting room/library, as well as patio nooks for reading and relaxing.

On the west edge of downtown, about 10 blocks due west of the *zócalo*, stands **Casa Colonial** (Calle Miguel Negrete 105, tel./fax 951/516-5280, toll-free U.S./Can. tel. 800/758-1697, www.casa-colonial.com, $45-110). Personable owner Jane Robison, who seems to know everyone in town, calls her 13-room domain the "posada with no sign," because she doesn't advertise and only accepts guests with reservations. Upon arrival, you immediately see why Casa Colonial is such a favorite among savvy visitors. Low-rise rooms and apartments envelop a spacious, gracefully lovely inner garden. Guests enjoy the use of a living room with a fine library and Wi-Fi. Room prices vary according to size and elegance; there's a 10 percent discount if you pay in cash. For information on Casa Colonial Tours, visit the website.

APARTMENTS

Many Oaxacans offer apartment or house rentals and lodging in their homes. If you're interested, be sure to see the classified sections of the English-language newspaper *Oaxaca Times,* either online (www.oaxacatimes.com) or at their editorial office (Macedonio Alcalá 307, tel. 516-3443), or check out the excellent website www.vrbo.com (Vacation Rentals by Owner). If you'd like to experience a homestay with a Mexican family, ask for information at one of the several Oaxaca language schools that arrange homestays.

Just three blocks from the *zócalo*, find the secluded and attractive, **Casa Luz María** (1002 Morelos, tel. 951/514-6280 or 951/516-2378, luzmago30@hotmail.com, $450/month for two). The sprightly, grandmotherly owner, who retired from running her lodging as a bed-and-breakfast, now offers four smallish furnished apartments around a pair of flowery interior patios. The apartments include a

HOSTELS

Oaxaca's best hostel might be the beautifully restored ★ **Paulina Youth Hostel** (V. Trujano 321, tel. 951/516-2005, www.paulinahostel.com, dorms $14 pp, rooms $27 s, $29 d, $44 t, $58 q), just three blocks west of the *zócalo*. The owners created the best of all possible hostelling worlds, with a good cafeteria and inviting, spacious common areas. With 100 beds in six private rooms and 10 dorms, the comfortable, squeaky-clean rooming options include separate male and female dorms and private rooms with shower-baths, all with comfortable orthopedic mattresses, roof terrace, hot water, and hearty breakfast thrown in for free. Get your reservations in early.

Also worthy are two hostels in the picturesque Los Arquitos neighborhood on the far northwest side of downtown. First, consider **Hostal Pochón** (Callejon del Carmen 102, tel. 951/516-1322, www.hostalpochon.com, dorms $12 pp, rooms $14-20 d, includes breakfast), two blocks west and nine blocks north (15 min.) from the *zócalo*'s northwest corner. The owners offer lodging for about 30 guests in three separate dorms, three rooms with shared bath, and one suite with private bath. Amenities include Wi-Fi, library, use of phone, cable TV, free popcorn, and more.

In the same northwest neighborhood is the very worthy **Posada Don Mario** (Cosijopi 219, tel./fax 951/514-2012, www.posadadonmario.com, rooms with shared bath $31 s, $41 d, $60 t, rooms with private bath $41 s, $54 d) on a quiet side street. Hardworking owner Norma Moran offers 10 rooms and a dormitory, tucked around an intimate downstairs patio and an airy upstairs porch, furnished with comfy chairs and couches for reading and relaxing. Continental breakfast and in-house Internet are included.

A number of hostels have opened on the north side in recent years, catering to the new generation of low-budget travelers who have discovered Oaxaca City's allure. Among the best, combining low prices, modern and comfortable facilities, and good location are the following pair: **Hostel Alcalá** (Valdivieso 120—this is the one block between the zócalo and Macedonio Alcalá not closed to traffic—tel. 951/501-0289, hostelalcala.hostel.com, dorms $8-11, private rooms $27 d, $35 t) offers dorm-style sleeping arrangements and a couple of private rooms for 2-3 people. Enter by climbing the spiral stairs at the back of Cafecito (same address). Secure lockers, Wi-Fi, table games, flat screen cable TV, and free coffee and continental breakfast come with the very low price of a bed.

Farther north and east find **Hostel Don Nino Oaxaca** (Pino Suarez 804, tel. 951/502-5336, hosteldonnino.com, dorms $12, private rooms and suites $38-50 s, $46-50 d, $60 t, all include breakfast) overlooking tranquil El Llano park. A modern hostel tucked into a vintage Oaxaca building, Don Nino's offers men's, women's, and mixed dorms and private rooms along with an on-site restaurant and bar, tour packages, a shared kitchen, table games, computers, Wi-Fi, and a terrace.

TRAILER PARKS AND CAMPING

The **Oaxaca Trailer Park** (900 Av. Violetas, tel. 951/515-0376, hookups $15, tents $10) lies at the far northeast side of town. Once a very popular facility, the Oaxaca Trailer Park has been partly converted to offices and apartments during the past few years. Nevertheless, it lives on, still with dozens of all-hookup spaces and tent spaces remaining. Amenities include big shade trees, diagonal parking spaces for the largest rigs, clean hot-water showers and toilets, a manager-watchperson, and the original sturdy security fence. Get there by turning left at Violetas, marked by the big green Colonia Reforma sign over the highway, a block or two past the baseball stadium, several blocks east of the first-class bus terminal on Highway 190. Continue uphill six long blocks to the trailer park entrance on the left.

Food

AROUND THE *ZÓCALO*
Cafés

Recent years have seen an explosion of coffee houses, shops, and bars all over Oaxaca City, along with cafés specializing in chocolate drinks and chocolate snacks of all kinds. The Oaxacan version of Starbucks is the **Italian Coffee Company** with several locations around town. The one with the best location is on the northeast corner of the *zócalo*, at Valdivieso and Hidalgo.

Snacks and Food Stalls

The cost of meals at many of Oaxaca's popular restaurants has risen during the past few years. Nevertheless, plenty of tasty, reasonably priced food is out there for the discerning diner to enjoy. Read on for a plethora of possibilities.

During fiestas, snack stalls along Hidalgo, at the cathedral-front Alameda de León square, abound with local delicacies. Choices include *tlayudas,* giant pizza-like crisp tortillas loaded with avocado, tomato, onions, and cheese; and *empanadas de amarillo,* huge tacos stuffed with cheese and red salsa. For dessert, have a *buñuelo,* a crunchy, honey-soaked wheat tortilla.

At non-fiesta times, you can still fill up on the sizzling fare of tacos, *tortas,* hamburgers, and hot dogs (eat 'em only when they are served hot) at stands that set up in the same vicinity, especially in the late afternoon and evenings.

Restaurants

Oaxaca visitors enjoy a number of reasonably priced eateries right on or near the *zócalo*. In fact, you could spend your entire time enjoying the fare of the several *zócalo*-front sidewalk cafés, but then, if you did, you'd miss out on the real story of Oaxacan cuisine, which is taking place a few blocks uptown.

But first, the *zócalo*. Of the eight cafés at street level, several offer recommendable food and service. Possibly the best of the lot is **Terranova** (tel. 951/516-4747) on the east side, for professionally prepared and served lunch and dinner entrées. For good, reasonably priced breakfasts, try **Primavera,** at the northwest (Hidalgo) corner. The adjacent west-side **La Cafetería** and **Del Jardín** (tel. 951/516-2092) rate OK for food, but their service can be spotty. **El Importador** (tel. 951/514-3200) is trying harder with entertaining, not-too-loud live music, and passably good food, at lower prices than neighboring Terranova. They all are open long hours, about 8am-midnight daily, and have typical menus: morning breakfasts ($2-5); soups and salads ($3-6); pasta, meat, poultry, and fish ($5-12).

As for *zócalo* restaurants with a view from upstairs, serious-eating longtimers return to **El Asador Vasco** (Portal Flores 10A on the 2nd Fl. balcony above Del Jardín, tel. 951/514-4755, 1pm-midnight daily, $25-35). The menu specializes in hearty Basque-style country cooking: salty, spicy, and served in the decor of a medieval Iberian manor house. Favorites include fondues (bean, sausage, and mushroom), garlic soup, salads, veal tongue, oysters in hot sauce, and the carnes asadas (roast meats) house specialties.

Longtimers also swear by the Oaxacan specialties at **Casa de la Abuela** (Grandmother's House; above the Primavera café, tel. 951/516-3544, 10am-11pm daily, $7-20) at the *zócalo*'s northwest corner. Here you can enjoy tasty, professionally prepared regional dishes and airy *zócalo* vistas from the balcony. Call for reservations and a table with a view.

For fine Oaxacan specialties in a graceful, old-world setting, try **Andariega Restaurant** (Independencia 503, tel./fax 951/514-9331, 7:30am-9pm daily, $8-14) in the Parador San Miguel, two blocks west of Catedral de Oaxaca. Here's one of your best chances to try some of Oaxaca's moles, such as *almendrado* (almond), *verde* (greena), *amarillo* (yellow), or *negro* (black), over chicken, beef, or pork. Other favorites are *chiles rellenos,* stuffed with cheese and *picadillo* (spiced meat), and red snapper in orange sauce. An excellent daily four-course *comida* (set lunch) runs about $8.

Moving uphill, the **Restaurant Catedral** (García Vigil 105, tel. 951/516-3285, 9am-midnight Mon.-Fri., 8am-2am Sat.-Sun., $8-16), two blocks north of the zócalo, at the corner of Morelos, serves as a tranquil daytime business and middle-to-upper-class refuge from the street hubbub. The refined ambience—music playing softly in the background, tables set around an airy, intimate fountain patio crowned by the blue Oaxaca sky above—is half the show. The finale is the attentive service and quality food for breakfast, lunch, or supper. The Aguilar family owners are especially proud of their moles that flavor their house specialties. These include fillets, both meat and fish, and regional dishes, such as banana leaf-wrapped tamales Oaxaqueños.

More good eating, in a genteel, relaxed atmosphere, awaits you at the very popular **Restaurant El Sagrario** (120 Valdivieso, tel. 951/514-0303 or 951/514-3319, 8am-midnight daily, $7-14), behind Oaxaca Cathedral. Mostly local, youngish, upper-class customers enjoy a club/bar atmosphere (lower level), pizza parlor booths (middle level), or restaurant tables (upper level). At the restaurant level, during the evening, you can best take in the whole scene around you—chattering, upbeat crowd; live guitar, flute, jazz, or salsa melodies; and elegantly restored colonial details. Then, finally, comes the food, beginning, perhaps, with an appetizer, continuing with a soup or salad, then an international or regional specialty, which you top off with a light dessert and a savory espresso. Music volume goes up later in the evening.

Groceries and Wine

For simple, straightforward grocery shopping, plus a small selection of good wines, go to handily located **Abarrotes Lonja** (8am-9:30pm daily), on the *zócalo*'s west side, next to La Cafetería café.

NORTH OF THE *ZÓCALO*
Cafés and Desserts

For coffee and dessert, you have a number of additional downtown choices, notably **Coffee Beans** (Cinco de Mayo 400, no phone, 8am-11pm daily), five blocks north of the *zócalo,* or nearby **Restaurant La Antigua** (a block east at Reforma 401, tel. 951/516-5761, noon-11pm daily, $3-8), just uphill from Abasolo.

A few blocks up Macedonio Alcalá find the tiny **Oaxacan Coffee Company** (100 Alcalá, no phone, 8am-9pm daily), serving organic brew and morning croissants. They also sell beans by the bag, and chocolate flavored with berries and spices. The service is take-out only. They also have main store and roasting facility (Constitución 108, tel. 951/218-1939). And for those who might be staying up in Xochimilco on the north side of Highway 190, the **A.M. Siempre Café** (Jose Lopez Alavez 1355, Xochimilco, tel. 951/515-6160, 8am-9pm daily) offers great coffee and pastries in the morning and sandwiches and lunch all day long. Try the chocolate cake—it's great!

An admirable coffee "chain" is ★ **Café Brújula** (various locations including García Vigil 409, 8am-10pm Mon.-Sat.; Macedonio Alcalá 104, no phone, 8am-10pm Mon.-Sat., 9am-10pm Sun.), roasting and serving coffee in Oaxaca since 2006. They work with the 21st of September Coop, which produces shade-grown organic coffee, and they roast their beans northern Italian style, good and dark. The shops are entertainingly decorated with visual puns, and the coffee is great.

Continue clockwise, north of the *zócalo* a block, to **Panadería Bamby** (northwest corner of García Vigil and Morelos, 6am-9pm Mon.-Sat.). A block east of the *zócalo,* stop by ★ **Pastelería and Café La Vasconia** (Independencia 907, between Cinco de Mayo and Reforma, tel. 951/516-2677, 8am-9pm daily, $2-6), with an inviting arched interior patio and a luscious selection of pastries, cakes, salads, and sandwiches. Another new addition to the many outstanding bakeries around the plaza is **Boulenc** (Porfirio Díaz 222-A, tel. 951/514-0582, 8:30am-8:30pm Mon.-Fri., 8:30am-5pm Sat., $1-7). The three young guys that run this place make great croissants in the morning, with or without chocolate, and pizzas, breads, chocolate chip cookes, and all kinds of great baked stuff all day long. For another kind of sweet treat, try ★ **Museo de las Nieves** (Alcalá 709-A at Humboldt, tel. 951/143-9253, museodelasnieves.com, $2 and up), where you can indulge in organic sorbet, ice cream, or gelato in all sorts of interesting flavors, not only the usual fruits and spices, but, say, cheese with basil and *mezcal* ice cream, or atun (cactus fruit) sorbet.

Snacks and Food Stalls

On the northwest side of downtown, take a look around the **Mercado Sánchez Pasqua** (8am-2pm Mon.-Sat.) for some pleasant surprises. (To get there, from the *zócalo* cathedral, walk uphill along García Vigil seven blocks to Humboldt and turn left a block to Porfirio Díaz. It's the market across the street, past the gigantic wild fig tree.) Here, you can enjoy the town's tastiest *comal* (charcoal-fired griddle) cooking. Enjoy a hearty, homestyle breakfast (perhaps *huevos a la mexicana* with hot tortillas, or hotcakes with honey and bacon).

For a special lunchtime treat, ask for ★ **Carmen Hernández Ramírez** and order her *memelas* (big, thick, open-face tortillas smothered in beans, $1.50) or the luscious, plump tamales ($1.50) of **Señora Catalina Minerva Paz.**

Much farther up the economic scale, sample the delicious offerings of ★ **Hostería Alcalá** (Macedonio Alcalá 307, 8:30am-11pm daily, $5-15), four blocks north of the *zócalo*. The airy, tranquil patio ambience is ideal for a relaxing refreshment or lunch break from sightseeing along the Macedonio Alcalá pedestrian mall.

Restaurants

Devotees of light, vegetarian-style (and economically priced) cuisine get what they're hungering for at ★ **La Manantial Vegetariana** (corner of west-side Calle Tinoco y Palacios 303, tel. 951/514-5602, 9am-9pm Mon.-Sat., lunch $6, dinner $8), located just north (uphill) of Matamoros, two blocks west and three blocks north of the *zócalo*. A tranquil patio ambience sets the tone for the house specialty, a set lunch *comida*. Typically they might offer soup (onion or cream of zucchini), salad (mixed greens or tomato cucumber), stew (mushroom or soya steak), bread, fruit drink, dessert, and coffee or tea.

Another northside budget vegetarian restaurant, **Calabacitas Tiernas** (Alcalá 802, tel. 951/201-2582, 1pm-5pm Mon.-Fri., 2pm-5pm Sat., $7), offers great, healthy lunch fare in the form of a five-course, fixed-price menu with fresh ingredients. This is a vegetarian and vegan oasis with a hip, young professional clientele.

Step into the unpretentiously elegant, vine-hung atrium-courtyard of the ★ **Hostería Alcalá** (307 Macedonio Alcalá, tel. 951/516-2093 or 951/514-0820, 8am-11pm Mon.-Sat., 7am-10pm Sun., $12-14), and choose from a long menu of professionally prepared and presented salads, soups, pasta, meats, and fish. The Hostería provides an invitingly cool and soothing refuge on a warm afternoon. Find it one block downhill from the Santo Domingo church-front.

Right across from the Santo Domingo church, enjoy some relief from high restaurant prices at **Nostrana** (Macedonio Alcalá 501A, tel. 951/514-0778, 1pm-11pm daily, $7-12). In the cozy, five-table, old-country Italian dining room, relax and choose from a long menu of genuine Napolitano (the owners are Italian immigrants) country cooking. Choices include prosciutto, salads, plenty of pizza, and superb pasta, all washed down by good red wine.

A few doors west of Nostrana you'll find ★ **Pitiona** (Allende 108, tel.951/514-0690, pitiona.com, $7-40), one of Oaxaca's most talked about new restaurants (a write-up in the *New York Times* didn't hurt). Yes, this stylish place could hold its own in New York, both visually and gastronomically. Nor is it low budget. But Oaxacan-born chef Jose Manuel Baños Rodriguez, from Pinotepa, is busy reinventing traditional Oaxacan cuisine in a lively new fashion. Venison with yellow mole, goat hip stew, river mussel tamales, and mango tacos with pear mousse are but a few of the unusual gems on this menu.

Around the corner from Pitiona on García Vigil—uptown Oaxaca's new "restaurant row"—find three more restaurants offering variations on this same theme of reinvented tradition. Call it Oaxacan fusion. First, **Zandunga** (García Vigil 512-E, tel. 951/516-2265, $3-$15), named for the beloved theme song from Oaxaca's isthmus, features contemporary versions of that regional cuisine. The pulled pork with potato puree is pure dining pleasure.

Second, don't miss **La Biznaga** (García Vigil 512, tel. 951/516-1800, labiznaga.com.mx, $6-12), home of very slow food, as the website proclaims. That's all right, it's a lively room, with plenty of mezcal options to sample while you wait for the slow food, which includes such delights as fried squash blossoms in poblano chile sauce, shrimp with garlic, chile, and tamarind mole, and an array of unique and original soups.

Last but not least, down the block find **Zicanda** (García Vigil 409-A, tel. 951/501-0715, $8-26), where cocinero (chef) Yiannis Roja Pozos works his magic in a visually stunning dining room with a glowing bar at the back featuring, of course, several dozen flavors and brands of mezcal. Try the grilled octopus, spicy watermelon salad, or plantain dumplings with mole negro.

If you're unfamiliar with (or unconvinced about) Oaxaca's mole sauces, erase your doubt by walking two blocks east of the front of Iglesia de Santo Domingo to **Restaurant los Pacos** (Abasolo 121, tel. 951/516-1704, 10am-10pm daily, $12-14). Your meal automatically comes with a mole appetizer sampler, which treats you to six—*coloradito, verde, negro, estofado, Amarillo,* and *chichilo*—of Oaxaca's moles right off the bat. It only gets better after that, especially if you continue with one of the good salads, from Caesar to tomato, then follow up with a traditional Oaxaca specialty, such as *enchiladas coloradito con picadillo, espinazo de puerco con mole verde,* or *entomatadas,* either *solas* (alone) or with beef.

Also behind Santo Domingo, half a block

art and design on display in lobby of the restaurant Zandunga

north of Abasolo, **Café La Olla** (Reforma 402, in front of Casa de las Bugambilias bed-and-breakfast, tel. 951/516-6668, 8am-10pm daily, $6-15) enjoys a loyal following of longtime North American residents and visitors. Here, the dark-beamed ceiling, subdued spotlighting of the art-decorated walls, quiet music, and candlelight set a refined, romantic tone. Select from a long but light menu of skillfully prepared and presented soups (Aztec soup is nearly a meal in itself), salads, Oaxacan specialties, and meats. (Café La Olla's main drawback is street noise, which you can minimize by taking an upstairs table.)

Right across the street is **Café La Antigua** (Reforma 401, tel. 951/516-5761, 9am-11pm Mon.-Sat., $3-10), enjoyed by a long list of loyal patrons for entirely different reasons. Here, the main course is conversation and fine on-site roasted Oaxaca "Pluma" coffee (from the farms around Pluma Hidalgo village, in the sierra above Huatulco). Along with their savory lattes, cold cappuccinos, and mocha frappés, patrons can enjoy fresh baked goods, crepes, sandwiches, eggs, and juices. The prime mover behind all this is friendly coffee grower and owner Diego Woolrich Ramírez.

A few blocks north and west of the *zócalo*, discriminating diners will seek out **Luvina Cocina de Taller** (Mártires de Tacubaya 517, tel. 951/132-5912, luvinaoaxaca.wix.com/luvina#!bar/c16fk, 1pm-11pm Tues.-Sat., 1pm-8pm Sun., $5-15), the dining "workshop" inspired by the writer Juan Rulfo. The space is light and wonderful, and the Oaxacan fusion menu offers yet another new expression of the meaning of Oaxacan cuisine. The location is in an alleyway off the small street called Cosijoeza, north of the street called La Constitición, and a little hard to find, but if you take the time you won't regret it.

Finally, if you're hankering for good seafood, take a table in the relaxing garden of northeast-side **Mariscos Jorge** (on Pino Suárez, across from El Llano park, tel. 951/513-4308, 8am-6:30pm daily, $8-16), the standout standby of local middle- and upper-class patrons. Choose from a long menu: 14 cocktail selections including shrimp, squid, and clams; salads and soups; and entrées, including fish fillets, from breaded and baked to *a la diabla*, octopus, and much more. It's also a good place to go for breakfast.

Due east of the south side of the *zócalo*, **Café Bistrot Epicuro** (Vicente Guerrero 318, tel. 951/514-9750, 1pm-11pm Wed.-Mon., $9-19) provides an Italian break from Oaxacan cuisine. Many claim Bistrot has the best pizza in Oaxaca, for what it's worth (and it's worth something, as there are quite a few pizza places here). They also serve pastas, Italian specialties (the owners are from Genoa), and some Mexican dishes as well. The room is so pretty and pleasant that the rooftop deck with its retractable roof goes unused at times.

Groceries, Wine, and Natural Food

Local devotees go to **Xiguela** café and natural food store (Hidalgo 104C, corner of Cinco de Mayo, in the northeast-side Jalatlaco district, no phone, 9am-6pm Mon.-Fri., 9am-3pm Sat.). There they stock up with healthy goodies, teas (arnica, anise, manzanilla), organic grains, granola, yogurt, honey, jams, and a ton more.

SOUTH OF THE ZÓCALO
Bakeries

For baked goods, try the sweet offerings of **Tartamiel Pastelería Frances** (on Trujano, half a block west from the southwest corner of the *zócalo*, tel. 951/516-7330, 7am-8pm Mon.-Sat., 8:30am-7pm Sun.).

Snacks and Food Stalls

For economical sit-down meals, visit the acre of food stalls inside the **Mercado 20 de Noviembre,** two blocks south and one block west of the *zócalo*'s southwest corner. Adventurous eaters will be in heaven among a wealth of succulent *chiles rellenos;* piquant moles; fat, banana leaf-wrapped *tamales Oaxaqueños;* and savory *sopas* (soups) and *guisados* (stews). Insist, however, that your selection be served hot.

Restaurants

Only a few good sit-down restaurants sprinkle the neighborhoods south of the *zócalo*. A trio of them, two well known for Oaxacan cuisine, and one for seafood, stand out.

Local folks strongly recommend the no-nonsense, country-style (but refined) **La Flor de Oaxaca** (Armenta y López 311, tel. 951/516-5522, 7:30am-10pm Mon.-Sat., 9am-3pm Sun., $8-10), a block east and half a block south from the *zócalo's* southeast corner. The mole-smothered regional specialties come mostly in four styles: *con tasajo* (thin broiled steak), *con pollo* (chicken), *con cecina* (roast pork), or *sola* (without meat). Besides those, you can choose from an extensive menu of equally flavorful items, such as *tamales Oaxaqueños* (wrapped in banana leaves), pork chops, several soups, spaghetti, and much more. Credit cards are accepted.

A block west and two blocks south of the *zócalo's* southwest corner, ★ **Restaurant Tayu** (20 de Noviembre 416, tel. 951/516-5363, 8am-6pm Mon.-Sat., $3-7) allows you to step in to Oaxaca "as it used to be." Take a table and relax in the refined, old-world, TV-free ambience. In the mornings, select from a host of tasty breakfasts; in the afternoons, choose one of their four-course $6 *comidas* that include a choice between several hearty entrées, such as short ribs, chicken, *chiles rellenos*, with soup, rice, and dessert included. Arrive in the afternoon, 2:30pm-4:30pm, and enjoy their live instrumental music.

Lovers of fresh seafood can join the loyal brigade of local folks who frequent the airy and unpretentious **Restaurant La Red** (The Net; corner of Bustamante and Colón, tel. 951/514-8840, noon-9pm daily, $10-16), one of five Oaxaca branches, located one block south of the *zócalo's* southeast corner. Customers get their heart's delight of generous seafood cocktails, heaping bowls of shrimp, fish fillets, octopus, and much more.

Fine Dining

The Oaxaca visitor influx during the 1990s nurtured a crop of fine restaurants. If at all possible, visit the elegant ★ **Los Danzantes** (Macedonio Alcalá 402, tel. 951/501-1184 or 951/501-1187, 1:30pm-11:30pm daily, $20 lunch, $35 dinner), where everything seems designed for perfection. We were lucky to enjoy a surprisingly economical ($10 until 6pm) set lunch, which, when offered, changes daily. In the airy dining atrium, beneath blue sky and sunlight filtering through curtains artfully draped overhead, waiters scurried, starting us off with chilled artichoke soup, and continuing with savory spinach lasagna with Oaxaca *requesón* cheese, accompanied by delicious pressed guava-apple juice. They topped it all off with delectable dark-Oaxaca chocolate mousse and espresso coffee. Bravo! After such an introduction, you'll be tempted to return on another day. Reservations are strongly recommended.

Hotel manager and chef Alejandro Ruiz of **Casa Oaxaca** (García Vigil 407, tel. 951/516-8889, $25-35) now has new venues to work his culinary wonders. While the Casa Oaxaca remains at its original address, the restaurant and its new sister café have moved to a couple of different locations. The vine-draped and breezily casual **Casa Oaxaca Café** (Jasmines 518, corner of. Sabinas, tel. 951/502-6017, casaoaxacacafe.com, $10-25) offers much of the same great cuisine as the restaurant, but opens for all three meals and charges slightly lower prices. Ruiz puts his all into blending the best of old and new cuisine at the elegant new location of the **Casa Oaxaca Restaurant** (Constitución 104-A, tel. 951/516-8531, casaoaxacaelrestaurante.com, 1pm-11pm Mon.-Sat., 1pm-9pm Sun., $23-30), with its rooftop bar. For example, start off with duck pâté and continue with *flor de calabaza*, stuffed with cheese and accompanied by *tostaditas* (toasted corn) and guacamole. Follow through with broiled shrimp in their juice with lentils, or baked *robalo* (snook) with lemon, all accompanied with a bottle of white wine from their extensive list. Finish off with baby coconut custard, mango pie, or *guanabana* mousse, or a sampling of all three. Reservations are mandatory.

In the far northeast corner of downtown, showplace **Restaurant La Toscana** (corner of Cinco de Mayo and Alianza, tel. 951/513-8742, 2pm-10pm daily, $10-20), in the old northeast-side Jalatlaco neighborhood, offers a long, elegant Mediterranean menu, spiced with a dash of traditional Oaxaca. Although it would be hard to go wrong with most anything here, I enjoyed the lettuce and tomato salad with goat cheese, shrimp fettuccine, leg of *jabalí* (wild pig), and, for dessert, croquettes of coconut and banana. Reservations are recommended. Note that this is a different Cinco de Mayo from the one near Santo Domingo—note as well that this restaurant is located in a beautifully fading old building with no signage.

Groceries, Wine, and Natural Food
For fruits and vegetables, the cheapest and freshest are in Mercado Juárez, which takes up the square block immediately southwest of the *zócalo*.

Information and Services

TOURIST INFORMATION
The state tourism secretariat maintains an **information office** (703 Av. Juárez, tel./fax 951/516-0123, www.aoaxaca.com, 8am-8pm daily) on the west side of El Llano park. They also staff a town center **information desk** (on Independencia, corner of García Vigil, tel. 951/516-5645, 10am-6pm Tues.-Sun.) at their former headquarters (now the Museum of Oaxacan Painters), at the north edge of the *zócalo*, half a block north of the cathedral-front.

Furthermore, the city (Coordinaciñn de Turismo Municipal) also maintains a town-center **tourist information office** (102 Matamoros, tel. 951/516-9901 or 951/516-8365, 9am-6pm Mon.-Sat.). Follow García Vigil two blocks north of the *zócalo*, turn left (west), and continue half a block.

Travel and Tour Agencies and Guides
Lohbi Tours and Travel (corner of Valdivieso and Independencia, tel. 951/514-3165, lohbitour@yahoo.com.mx, 9am-2pm Mon.-Sat.), one block northeast of the *zócalo*, behind the cathedral, is a good source for most travel services, especially air tickets.

Other agencies are likewise experienced, especially with tours. Among them is **Viajes Xochitlán** (García Vigil 617, tel. 951/514-3271, www.xochitlan-tours.com.mx, 9am-2pm and 4pm-7pm Mon.-Sat.). Travel in comfort to Oaxaca City and Valley sites and villages, such as Monte Albán, Mitla, Teotitlán del Valle, Tlacolula, and much more. They specialize in individuals and groups, tourist and business services, and travel agent services, such as air and bus tickets and hotel bookings.

Another reliable, long-time travel and tour agent is **Viajes Turísticos Mitla** (Mina 501, tel. 951/516-6175 or 951/501-0220). The office is three blocks west and three blocks south of the *zócalo*'s southwest corner, near the departure points for several tour bus companies. They also provide very economical bus-only tourist transportation to a plethora of Valley of Oaxaca sites, with multiple daily departures to Monte Albán.

There are literally dozens of these tour agencies around downtown Oaxaca, all offering tours for small to medium-sized groups, usually on a given schedule that covers 3-6 Oaxaca Valley destinations in a half- or full-day of touring with a bilingual guide. Given Oaxaca's not-so-great traffic management and the cost of a rental car, this is probably the best and most economical way to see the sights in the Valley of Oaxaca. The prices are generally in the $12-15 price range for a four- to six-hour tour, but this does not include entry fees at the destinations, or the price of lunch at a restaurant of the driver's choosing.

A Oaxaca regiment of **private individual guides** also offers tours. Among the most highly recommended is the fluent-in-English **Juan Montes Lara** (Prol. de Eucaliptos 303, Colonia Reforma, tel./fax 951/513-0126, jmonteslara@yahoo.com, $25/hour), backed up by his wife Karin Schutte. Besides cultural sensitivity and extensive local knowledge, Juan and Karin also provide comfortable transportation in a big Chrysler van.

Moreover, satisfied customers rave about guide **Sebastian Chino Peña** (home tel. 951/562-1761, cell tel. 044-951/508-1220 in Oaxaca City, sebastian_oaxaca@hotmail.com, $20/hour). He offers tours by car of anywhere you would like to go in the city or valley of Oaxaca.

More athletic travelers might enjoy the services of **Zona Bici** (García Vigil 409, tel. 951/516-0953, www.bikeoaxaca.com), five blocks due north of the *zócalo*, which rents bikes and also conducts bike tours into the countryside.

For even more extensive backcountry adventure bicycling, hiking, and camping in the mountains just north of the Valley of Oaxaca, contact **Expediciones Sierra Norte** (M. Bravo 210, tel./fax 951/514-8271, www.sierranorte.org.mx).

You might inquire for a guide recommendation at the state tourist **information office** (703 Av. Juárez, tel./fax 951/516-0123, www.aoaxaca.com, 8am-8pm daily). They maintain a list of officially-sanctioned and certified guides.

HEALTH AND EMERGENCIES

If you get sick, ask your hotel desk to recommend a doctor. Otherwise, go to the 24-hour **Clinica Hospital Carmen** (Abasolo 215, tel./fax 951/516-0027), staffed by English-speaking IAMAT Doctors Horacio Tenorio S. and Germán Tenorio V. Alternatively, go to the highly-recommended northside **Hospital Reforma** (Reforma 613, tel. 951/516-6100), a block west of El Llano park.

For routine medicines and drugs, go to one of many pharmacies, such as the **Farmacia Ahorros** (on Cinco de Mayo, near the northeast corner of Murguia, 7am-11pm daily), one block east and two blocks north of the cathedral. After hours, call Farmacia Ahorros's free **24-hour delivery service** (tel. 951/515-5000). Most pharmacies in Oaxaca, indeed in all of Mexico, have on staff at least one pharmacist who is well-versed in medicine, and can help you figure out what ails you and what you need to cure it.

For fire or police emergencies, call the **emergency number 066**, or take a taxi to the municipal **police station** (*policia municipal*; Morelos 108, tel. 951/516-0455), or call the **firefighters** (*bomberos*; tel. 951/506-0248).

BOOKSTORES AND PUBLICATIONS

The best source for English-language books about Mexico is the **Librería Amate** (Alcalá 307, ground floor of Plaza Alcalá, tel. 951/516-6960, fax 951/516-7181, www.amatebooks.com, 10am-8:30pm Mon.-Sat., 2pm-7pm Sun.), four blocks north of the *zócalo*.

The interesting **Librería de Bibliofiles de Oaxaca** (Bibliophiles' Bookstore of Oaxaca; Macedonio Alcalá 104, tel. 951/516-9901, 10am-9pm daily), downhill from Iglesia de Santo Domingo, offers a big collection of new, mostly Spanish books, with a good number of art, crafts, archaeology, and cultural books in English.

Pick up a copy of the good daily English-language *News*, from Mexico City, available late mornings, except Sunday, at the newsstand near the *zócalo*'s southwest corner, a few steps south on Cabrera.

Also, you can print out copies of the useful tourist newspapers, *Oaxaca Times* (www.oaxacatimes.com) and *Go-Oaxaca* (www.go-oaxaca.com) on the Internet. Pick up the *Oaxaca Times* paper edition at hotels, shops, travel agents, the local tourist information offices, or at the publisher (Macedonio Alcalá 307, upstairs, tel./fax 951/516-3443).

MONEY EXCHANGE

Several banks, all with ATMs, sprinkle the downtown area. (*Note:* Remove your ATM card promptly; some local machines are known to "eat" them if left in for more than about 15 seconds after the transaction is finished.) One of the most convenient is the **Banamex ATM** (on Valdivieso, directly behind Oaxaca Cathedral, 9am-4pm Mon.-Fri.). As of this writing, many ATMs in Mexico are frequently the targets of fraud, as in guys who'll set up the machine to steal your PIN and then drain your account. We recommend using ATMs located inside or adjacent to banks, where access is controlled.

The best-bet, full-service bank with long hours is **HSBC** (one block north, one block east of the *zócalo* corner of Guerrero and Armenta y López, tel. 951/514-7040 or 951/516-9754, 8am-6pm Mon.-Fri., 9am-6pm Sat.).

A full-service **Banamex** branch (Hidalgo at Cinco de Mayo, tel. 951/516-5900, 9am-4pm Mon.-Sat.) nearby receives customers just one block due east of the *zócalo*. If Banamex is too crowded, go to HSBC or **Banco Santander** (on the Independencia corner, north of the Oaxaca Cathedral, tel. 951/516-1100, 9am-4pm Mon.-Sat.); they change U.S. and Euro currencies and travelers checks.

If banks are closed, try moneychanger **Ce Cambio** (on Valdivieso, corner of Independencia, tel. 951/516-3399, 9am-6pm Mon.-Fri., 9am-5pm Sat.), just north of the *zócalo,* behind the Oaxaca Cathedral. Although it may pay about a percent less than the banks, it changes many major currencies. There are numerous other money changers on most of the streets around the *zócalo,* all offering pretty much the same services at the same rates. If you have the option, you'll do better withdrawing cash from an American account from a safely located ATM, since you'll get the bank rate rather than the money changer rate. And within reason, take as much money out as you need, since you'll pay the same fee for a 1,000-peso withdrawal as you will for a 5,000-peso withdrawal.

COMMUNICATIONS

The Oaxaca **post office** (*correo;* corner of Alameda de León plaza and Independencia, tel. 951/516-1291, 8am-7pm Mon.-Fri., 10am-5pm Sat.) is across from the cathedral-front. Mail service in and from Mexico ranges from abominable to painfully slow. Don't rely on it for anything important. A block west of the post office, the **telecomunicaciones** (corner of Independencia and 20 de Noviembre, tel. 951/516-4902, 8am-7:30pm Mon.-Fri., 9am-4pm Sat., 9am-noon Sun.) offers money orders, telephones, and public fax machines.

For long-distance and local telephone service, buy a Ladatel phone card (widely available in stores; look for the yellow Ladatel sign) and use it in public street telephones.

Answer your email and access the Internet at any one of a number of spots around the *zócalo*. For example, try the small shop behind the cathedral (Valdevieso 120, tel. 951/514-9227, 9am-11pm daily). Most Oaxaca hotels have free Wi-Fi, though it may be a little slow and you might have to sit near the reception desk.

LIBRARIES

Visitors starving for a good read in English will find satisfaction at the **Oaxaca Lending Library** (Pino Suárez 519, tel. 951/518-7077, www.oaxlibrary.org, 10am-2pm and 4pm-7pm Mon.-Fri., 10am-1pm Sat.), about five blocks north of the *zócalo* on the west side of Pino Suárez, a block north of Constitución.

The city **biblioteca** (public library; corner of Morelos and Macedonio Alcalá, tel. 951/516-1853, 9am-8:30pm Mon.-Fri., 10am-2pm Sat.), two blocks north of the *zócalo* in a lovingly restored former convent, is worth a visit, if only for its graceful, cloistered Renaissance interiors and patios. The library holdings are nearly all in Spanish.

CONSULATES AND IMMIGRATION

The **U.S. Consulate** (Macedonio Alcalá 407, tel. 951/514-3054 or 951/518-2853, fax 951/516-2701, 11am-4pm Mon.-Thurs.) is upstairs at Plaza Santo Domingo, across from the Santo Domingo church. In an emergency, call the **U.S. Embassy** (tel. 01-55/5080-2000). The **Canadian Consulate** (700 Pino Suárez, local 11B, tel. 951/513-3777, fax 951/515-2147, 11am-2pm Mon.-Fri.) services Canadian citizens. In an emergency, call the **Canadian Embassy in Mexico City** (toll-free Mex. tel. 800/706-2900).

Other consulates that may be available in Oaxaca are the **Italian Consulate** (Macedonio Alcalá 400, tel. 951/516-5058) and the **Spanish Consulate** (Porfirio Díaz 340, Colonia Reforma, tel. 951/515-3525 or 951/518-0031). For more information, look for consulate contact numbers in the *Oaxaca Times* or the telephone directory Yellow Pages, under *Embajadas, Legaciones, y Consulados,* or call the U.S. or Canadian consulates for information.

If you lose your tourist permit, make arrangements with **Migración** (at the airport, tel. 951/511-5733, 7am-9pm daily) at least several hours before your scheduled departure from Mexico. Bring with you proof of your arrival date in Mexico—stamped passport, airline ticket, or copy of the lost permit.

LAUNDRY

Get your laundry done at conveniently located **Super Lavandería** (corner of Hidalgo and J. P. Garcia, tel. 951/514-1181, 8am-8pm Mon.-Sat.), two blocks west of the *zócalo*'s northwest corner.

PHOTOGRAPHY

Good photo stores in downtown Oaxaca include **Foto Figueroa** (Hidalgo 516, corner 20 de Noviembre, tel. 951/516-3766, 9am-8pm Mon.-Sat.). With plenty of Kodak digital accessories, it offers quick digital and develop-and-print services. Another store with the same range of services and accessories is **Central Fotografia** (Rayón 117, tel. 951/514-4479, 951/516-9517, 9am-6pm Mon.-Sat., closed Sun.).

VOLUNTEER WORK AND DONATIONS

Local residents and visitors have banded together to provide help for Oaxaca's street children and poor single-parent families. A formerly grassroots organization, **Centro de Esperanza Infantile** (Crespo 308, tel. 951/501-1069, www.oaxacastreetchildrengrassroots.org, 9am-4pm Mon.-Fri., 9am-2pm Sat.) operates cooperatively out of its center, about four blocks north and three blocks west of the *zócalo*. The all-volunteer organization raises money for food, schoolbooks and uniforms, housing, foster care, and much more for homeless children and destitute single mothers and their children. They welcome donations and volunteers, and visitors are always welcome. Check the website for an address for sending donations within the United States or Canada.

LANGUAGE INSTRUCTION AND COURSES

A long list of satisfied clients attest to the competence of the language instruction of the **Instituto Cultural de Oaxaca** (northside corner of Calz. Niños Héroes/Hwy. 190 and Av. Juárez, tel. 951/515-3404, fax 951/515-3728, www.icomexico.com), in a lovely garden campus.

Also very highly recommended is the **Becari Language School** (M. Bravo 210, tel./fax 951/514-6076, www.becari.com.mx). Offerings include small-group Spanish instruction, as well as cooking and dancing classes. If you desire, the school can arrange homestays with local families.

Similarly experienced is the **Vinigulaza Language and Tradition School** (Vinigulaza Idioma y Tradición; Abasolo 503, corner of Los Libres, about six blocks east, four blocks north of the plaza, tel. 951/513-2763, www.vinigulaza.com), associated with the local English-language Cambridge Academy. Offerings include informative (and even fun), small-group Spanish instruction. Schedules are flexible, and prices are reasonable.

Alternatively, for more lightweight instruction, try **Español Interactivo** (Interactive Spanish; Armenta y López 311B, tel./fax 951/514-6062, www.studyspanishinoaxaca.com), one block east and half a block south of the *zócalo*, by Iglesia de San Agustín. The school offers several levels that provide 15-40 instructional hours per week. Classes have a maximum of five students.

All the language schools also arrange **homestays** with Oaxaca families and often offer classes in folkloric and salsa dancing, weaving, and painting on clay and wood.

Inexpensive Spanish instruction is customarily available from volunteers at the **Oaxaca Lending Library** (Pino Suárez 519, tel. 951/518-7077, www.oaxlibrary.org), about five blocks north of the *zócalo* and a block north (uphill) from Constitución.

OAXACAN COOKING AND CULTURE

Susana Trilling, Oaxaca resident and author of *My Search for the Seventh Mole* (as in MOH-lay), offers an unusual mix of Oaxacan culture, cooking, and eating, with a lodging option, at her **Seasons of My Heart cooking school** (Rancho Aurora; in Oaxaca, local cell tel. 044-951/508-0469; in Mexico, long-distance 045-951/508-0469; from Canada or U.S. 011-52-1-951/508-0469; www.seasonsofmyheart.com) in the Etla Valley, north of the city. Susana's simplest offering is a half-day cooking lesson ($50). She also offers a one-day group cooking adventure ($75), which includes a morning trip to a local native market to buy food, then preparing and eating at Susana's ranch. Farther-ranging cooking courses (six days, $1,500) regularly include trips to outlying parts of Oaxaca, such as the Isthmus of Tehuántepec or northern Oaxaca, around Tuxtepec.

Transportation

AIR

The Oaxaca airport (code-designated OAX) has several daily flights that connect with Mexico City and other Mexican and international destinations. Many of the Mexico City flights allow same-day connections between Oaxaca and many U.S. gateways.

Continental Airlines, (toll-free in Mex. tel. 800/900-5000) fortunately, has eliminated the stop in Mexico City en route to Oaxaca and now flies nonstop to and from Houston (flight time only 2.5 hours).

Aeroméxico (reservations toll-free in Mex. tel. 800/021-4000, tel. 951/516-1066, 951/516-7101, or 951/516-3765; flight information tel. 951/511-5055 or 951/511-5044) has flights that connect daily with Mexico City.

Budget carrier **Volaris Airlines** (toll-free in Mex. tel. 800/122-8000 and 800/865-2747) currently offers a direct Tijuana-Oaxaca connection, which is especially handy for southern California travelers.

Alternatively, light charter airlines (in the general aviation terminal, the building to the right as you face the main terminal) connect Oaxaca City with various points within Oaxaca. **Aerotucan** (tel. 951/502-0840, toll-free in Mex., outside Oaxaca tel. 800/640-4148, www.aerotucan.com.mx) regularly connects Oaxaca City with Puerto Escondido, Huatulco, and sometimes with Tuxtla Gutiérrez and Puebla.

The Oaxaca airport provides a modicum of services, such as a few shops for last-minute purchases; an international newsstand (seasonally only) with magazines and paperback novels; car rentals; a cafeteria in the waiting/boarding area, a mailbox (*buzón;* downstairs by the staircase to the restaurant); public Ladatel card-operated telephones; and an ATM downstairs.

Travel to and from the Airport

Arrival transportation for the 10-kilometer (six mi) trip into town is easy, aside from traffic jams. Buy tickets at the booth at the far right end of the terminal as you exit. Fixed-fare *colectivo* (shared taxi) tickets run about $5 per person for downtown ($7 to northside Hotels Misión de los Angeles, Fortín Plaza, and Victoria). For the same trip, a *taxi especial* (private taxi) ticket runs about $15 for four people; larger Nissan Vans cost $17 and $28 (depending on destination) for up to eight passengers. No public buses run between the airport and town.

Car rental agents stationed regularly at the Oaxaca airport are: **Alamo** (tel. 951/511-8534, toll-free in Mex. tel. 800/002-5266, tel./fax 951/514-8534, oaxalamo@hotmail.com); **Europcar** (tel. 951/516-8258, 951/516-9305 or 951/143-8340, toll-free in Mex. tel. 800/201-1111 or 800/201-2089, Oaxaca office Matamoros tel. 951/516-9305, www.europcar.com.mx), and **Economy Rent a Car** (Oaxaca office Cinco de Mayo 203, tel. 951/514-8534, economyrentacar.com). Economy offered the best prices on our last go-round and their employee pointed out to us that if you rent in town instead of at the airport, you pay 10 percent less. This is worth knowing if you are renting for more than a few days.

For **departure,** save taxi money by getting your *colectivo* airport transportation ticket ahead of time, at **Transportacion Terrestres** (on the west side of Plaza Alameda de León, across from the cathedral, tel. 951/514-4350, 9am-2pm and 5pm-8pm Mon.-Sat.).

If you lose your tourist permit, take proof of your arrival date in Mexico, such as a stamped passport, airline ticket, or copy of lost permit, to airport **Migración** (tel. 951/511-5733, 8am-9pm daily) a minimum of several hours prior to departure from Mexico.

CAR OR RV

Paved (but long, winding, and sometimes potholed) roads connect Oaxaca City with all regions of Oaxaca and neighboring states.

Four routes connect Oaxaca City south to the Pacific coast; two of them, via Highways 175 and 131, connect directly south over the super-scenic but rugged Sierra Madre del Sur. Especially during the June-October rainy season, travelers are subject to landslides and bridge washout delays. The longer but less rugged (and most dependable in bad weather) route connects Oaxaca via Highway 190 southeast to Tehuántepec, and from there to the Pacific coast Highway 200 west. The fourth route, also less direct, but still rugged and winding, travels west from Oaxaca, via Highway 190, and then south to the Pacific coast, via Highway 125.

The most direct route, narrow national **Highway 175,** runs along 238—winding, sometimes potholed—kilometers (148 mi), with its junction with coast Highway 200 at Pochutla (from there, it's 10 km/6 mi to Puerto Ángel). The road climbs to more than 2,700 meters (9,000 ft.) through winter-chilly pine forests and indigenous Chatino and Zapotec villages. Under dry, daylight conditions, count on about seven hours at the wheel if heading south from Oaxaca to Puerto Ángel, or about eight hours in the opposite direction. This is not a white-knuckle drive—not quite.

About the same is true for the paved **National Highway 131** route south from Oaxaca, which splits off of Highway 175 three kilometers (two mi) south of San Bartolo Coyotepec. On your way out of town, fill up with gasoline at the Oaxaca airport Pemex. Continue, via Zimatlán and Sola de Vega (fill up with gas again), over the pine-clad Pacific crest, a total of 254 kilometers (158 mi) to Puerto Escondido. Under dry, daylight conditions, allow about seven hours southbound, or about eight hours in the opposite direction. Gasoline is available mid-route at the Sola de Vega Pemex.

Highway 190 connects Oaxaca City southeast with Tehuántepec, along 250 kilometers (155 mi) of well-maintained but winding highway. Allow about 4.5 hours to Tehuántepec (downhill), or 5 hours in the opposite direction.

At Tehuántepec, connect west with Highway 200, via Salina Cruz, to the Oaxaca Pacific coast, and Bahías de Huatulco (161 km/100 mi, three hours), Pochutla-Puerto Ángel (200 km/124 mi, four hours), and Puerto Escondido (274 km/170 mi, five hours) via paved, lightly-traveled but secure **Highway 200.** All of the roads in coastal Oaxaca are undergoing great improvements as the tourism industry seeks to bring more people in, and these are, for the most part, easy drives.

The very long but super-scenic 368-kilometer (229 mi) **Highway 190-Highway 125** route connects Oaxaca southwest with coastal Pinotepa Nacional, via the Mixtec country destinations of Yanhuitlán, Teposcolula, and Tlaxiaco. Although winding most of the way, the generally uncongested road is safely drivable (subject to some potholes, however) from Oaxaca in about 10 driving hours if you use the *cuota autopista* northwest of Oaxaca City (exit to old Highway 190 at Nochixtlán). Add an hour for the 2,100-meter (7,000 ft.) climb in the opposite direction.

The 564-kilometer (350 mi) winding **Highway 190-Highway 160** from Oaxaca to Cuernavaca, Morelos, and Mexico City via Huajuapan de León requires a very long day, or better two days for safety. Under the best of conditions, the Mexico City-Oaxaca driving time runs 11 hours either way. Take it easy and stop overnight en route. (Make sure you arrive in Mexico City on a day when your car is permitted to enter. There are restrictions in place to reduce smog and traffic congestion in the city.)

Alternatively, you can cut your Mexico City-Oaxaca driving time significantly via the Mexico City-Puebla-Oaxaca *autopista*, combined 150D-131D, which, southbound, takes off from the southeast end of Mexico City's Calzada General Ignacio Zaragoza. Northbound, follow the signs on Highway 190 a few miles north of Oaxaca. Allow about six hours driving time at a steady 100 kph (60 mph). Tolls, which are worth it for the increased speed and safety, run about $30 for a car, much more for a big RV.

Car Rentals

Car rentals offer a convenient means of exploring Oaxaca City and environs. Although town and valley roads present no unusual hazards, drive defensively, anticipate danger, and keep a light foot on the accelerator. Also be aware that road hazards—animals, people, potholes, barricades, rocks—are much more dangerous at night. Traffic in Oaxaca City is like traffic in every city these days: slow-moving. Renting a car is not recommended if your itinerary is limited to Oaxaca City and the Valley of Oaxaca. Let tour company drivers do the work.

To rent a car, all you need is a current driver's license and a credit card. However, car rentals, which by law must include adequate Mexican liability insurance—that extra $12 a day you have pay, no matter what credit card you have—are expensive, running upwards of $40 per day in high season. Save *mucho dinero* by splitting the tariff with others. Rent in town instead of the airport and save 10 percent.

Get your rental through either a travel agent or, before departure, through U.S. and Canadian toll-free car rental numbers, or in Oaxaca locally: **Alamo** (tel. 951/511-6220, tel./fax 951/514-8534, fax 951/514-8686, Alamo.com); **Europcar** (at airport, or at Matamoros 101, tel./fax 951/143-8340, toll-free tel. in Mexico 800/201-1111 or 800/201-2084, europcar.com); **Economy Rent a Car** (at airport and at Cinco de Mayo 203, tel. 951/514-8534, toll-free 01-800/002-5266, economyrentacar.com).

VAN

Eight-to-sixteen-passenger vans, although less comfortable than first-class buses, provide faster service (at a much cheaper price). They are becoming increasingly popular for medium-distance connections, especially for the Pacific coast destinations of Pochutla-Puerto Ángel and Huatulco, northwest destinations in the Mixteca, and Northern Oaxaca destinations in the Sierra Norte, the Cañada, and around Tuxtepec.

At least two operators provide Oaxaca-Pochutla connections, from stations about one block east, three blocks south of the *zócalo*'s southeast corner. The first option is **Eclipse 70** (tel. 951/516-1068, Pochutla $12), which departs about every half hour during the day from Armenta y López 540. Alternatively, around the second left downhill corner, you can ride **Atlantida** (Noria 101, tel. 951/514-7077, $12) every two hours for the same price.

For a direct Huatulco connection, try competent carrier **Van 2000** (Hidalgo 208, westside, near Soledad Church, tel. 951/516-3154), which offers about eight daily departures, connecting with Crucecita on the Huatulco coast.

The northwest (Nochixtlan, Teposcolula, Tlaxiaco, Putla) van connection is **Excelencia** (Díaz Ordaz 305, tel. 951/516-3578), three blocks west, one block south, from the *zócalo*'s southwest corner.

For northern Cañada (Cuicatlan and Teotitlan del Camino) and Sierra Mazateca (Huautla de Jiménez) destinations, go by **Transportes Turistico Oaxaca-Cañada** vans (600 Trujano, five blocks west of the *zócalo,* tel. 951/378-1080).

BUS
Luxury and First Class

In contrast to vans, buses are much more comfortable and remain a popular option, especially for longer trips. Oaxaca's major luxury- and first-class carriers, Autobuses del Oriente and Omnibus Cristóbal Colón and their associated minor carriers, operate out of their terminal (toll-free in Mex. tel. 800/702-8000, Calz. Héroes de Chapultepec 1036, at Carranza, on the north side of town) on Highway 190. Bus lines accept credit cards for luxury- and first-class bookings. Passengers enjoy some amenities, such as Ladatel-card public telephones (on the terminal south end), snack stands, luggage lockers, air-conditioned first- and luxury-class waiting rooms, and cool, refined Restaurant Colibri across the street.

Moreover, all of the carriers that use the Héroes de Chapultepec terminal cooperate through the joint agency **Boletotal** (formerly Ticket Bus, toll-free in Mex. tel. 800/702-8000 or 800/009-9090, www.boletotal.com.mx, 8am-10pm Mon.-Sat. and 8am-9pm Sun.), which sells tickets at three town-center offices: on the *zócalo*'s south side, by the **Internet store** (tel. 951/513-3773); a block west of the *zócalo* (20 de Noviembre 103D, tel. 951/514-6655); and behind the Oaxaca Cathedral (corner of Independencia, tel. 951/502-0560).

Omnibuses Cristóbal Colón (OCC) offers first- and luxury-class connections with many Oaxaca and national destinations. Buses connect northwest with the Mixteca destinations of Nochixtlán, Tamazulapan, and Huajuapan de León, then continuing on to Puebla and Mexico City. Westerly, they connect with the Mixteca Alta, via Teposcolula, Tlaxiaco, Juxtlahuaca, Putla de Guerrero, and Pinotepa Nacional. Southerly, they connect (via the surer, but 11-hour long, Isthmus route) via Salina Cruz, with Huatulco, Pochutla-Puerto Ángel, and Puerto Escondido; and southeasterly, with Tehuántepec, Juchitán, Tapachula, Tuxtla Guitiérrez, and San Cristóbal de las Casas.

Autobuses del Oriente (ADO) also offers both first- and luxury-class Oaxaca connections, mostly along the Highway 190 corridor. First-class buses connect northwest with Mexico City (Tapo Tasqueña and Norte stations), via Nochixtlán and Huajuapan de León, and southeast with Tehuántepec and Salina Cruz. Other departures connect northeast with Coatzacoalcos, Villahermosa, Palenque, and Mérida; others connect north, with Tuxtepec, Veracruz, and Tampico.

ADO luxury-class buses mostly connect with Mexico City: ADO Platino (Platinum-class) connects, nonstop northwest, with Mexico City's Tapo and Norte stations, and southeast, with Tuxtla Gutiérrez in Chiapas. Furthermore, ADO GL luxury-class buses connect northwest, with Mexico City's Tapo and Tasqueño stations; southeast, with Tuxtla Gutiérrez and San Cristóbal de las Casas; and north, with Veracruz.

Also, first-class **Estrella de Oro** departures connect with Acapulco, via Huajuapan de León in the Mixteca, and Chilapa and Chipancingo in Guerrero.

Regional first-class **Cuenca** buses connect with northern Oaxaca points along Highway 175, including Ixtlán de Juárez, Valle Nacional, Tuxtepec, and Tierra Blanca, continuing all the way to Veracruz.

Note: Although first-class **Sur** and **Autobuses Unidos** (AU) tickets for reserved seats are sold at the Héroes de Chapultepec first-class station, they nevertheless depart from the Oaxaca Second-Class terminal. (Be sure to double-check your departure station when you buy Sur or AU tickets.)

Sur departures connect with Mexico City's Tapo station, along old Highways 190 and 160, via Huajuapan de León, Izucar de Matamoros, Puebla, and Cuatla, Morelos.

Autobuses Unidos departures connect with either Mexico City along the fast *autopista* expressway via Nochixtlán, Coixtlahuaca, and Puebla; or along the old Highway 131 via Cuicatlán, Teotitlán del Camino, Tehuacán, and Puebla.

Second Class

A swarm of long-distance second-class buses runs from the *camionera central segunda clase* (second-class bus terminal), southwest of downtown, just north of the Abastos market. Get there by taxi or by walking due west about eight blocks from the *zócalo* to the west end of Calle Las Casas. Take care crossing the busy *periférico* straight across the railroad tracks. Keep walking the same direction, along the four-lane street for two more blocks, to the terminal gate on the right. Inside, you'll find an orderly array of snack stalls, a cafeteria, luggage lockers, a long-distance telephone and fax, and a lineup of *taquillas* (ticket booths).

With one exception all ticket booths line up along the terminal to your left as you enter. **Fletes y Pasajes** (tel. 951/516-2270) dominates the terminal, with three separate ticket booths. All three Fletes y Pasajes booths sell tickets to most of their destinations. They offer very broad second-class service, connecting with nearly everywhere in Oaxaca except north: westerly, with Mixteca destinations of Nochixtlán, Tamazulapan, Huajuapan, and Tlaxiaco, connecting all the way via Highway 125 to Pinotepa Nacional on the coast; easterly, with Mitla and Mixe destinations of Ayutla, Zacatepec, and Juquila Mixes; and southeasterly, with Isthmus destinations of Tehuántepec, Juchitán, and Salina Cruz. Besides all of the above, Fletes y Pasajes offers luxury-class "super" expressway connections with Mexico City.

In approximate consecutive order, moving left from the entrance, first find **Transportes Oaxaca Istmo** (tel. 951/516-3664). Departures connect with dozens of destinations east and south. These include the east Valley of Oaxaca destinations of Tlacolula and Mitla, continuing to the Isthmus destinations of Tehuántepec, Juchitán, and Salina Cruz. From Tehuántepec and Salina Cruz, they connect west, with the Pacific coast destinations of Huatulco, Pochutla-Puerto Ángel, and Puerto Escondido.

Cooperating **Auto Transportes Oaxaca-Pacífico** (tel. 951/516-2908) and **Autobuses Estrella del Valle** travel the Highway 175 north-south route between Oaxaca and

Pochutla-Puerto Ángel. Both lines continue, connecting along east-west coastal Highway 200 with Bahías de Huatulco, Puerto Escondido, and Pinotepa Nacional.

Estrella Roja del Sureste and **Trans Sol** (tel. 951/516-0694), with some first-class buses, connect directly with Puerto Escondido along Highway 131 north-south via Sola de Vega (with a side-trip to Juquila pilgrimage shrine). From Puerto Escondido, you can make coastal connections with Pochutla-Puerto Ángel, Bahías de Huatulco, Jamiltepec, and Pinotepa Nacional.

Several other semi-local lines connect mostly with Valley of Oaxaca points: **Choferes del Sur,** with the northwest Valley of Oaxaca, ranging from San Felipe del Agua north of the city to Etla northwest; **Autobuses de Oaxaca** connects south with Cuilapan and Zaachila; and **Sociedad Cooperativa Valle del Norte** connects west with Teotitlán del Valle and Tlacolula. Lastly, if you hanker for a long, sometimes rough but scenic back-roads adventure, ride **Flecha de Zempoaltépetl** northeast to the remote Zapotec mountain native market towns of Villa Alta and Yalalag, via Tlacolula and Cuajimoloyas.

Finally, to the right of the entrance as you enter, **Pasajeros Benito Juárez** buses climb the mountains edging the Valley of Oaxaca's north side to the cool, pine-shadowed mountain-top communities of Benito Juárez and Cuajimoloyas (koo-ah-hee-moh-LO-yahs).

The Valley of Oaxaca

The Textile Route 59
The Crafts Route 70

Monte Albán and the
Archaeological Route 77

The cultural and economic riches of the city of Oaxaca flow largely from its surrounding hinterland, the Valley of Oaxaca, a mountain-rimmed patchwork expanse of fertile summer-green (and winter-dry) fields, pastures, and reed-lined rivers and streams. The Valley of Oaxaca consists of three subvalleys—the Valley of Tlacolula, the Valley of Ocotlán, and the Valley of Etla—that each extend about 30 miles east, south, and northeast of Oaxaca City. It is unique in a number of ways. Most important, the inhabitants are nearly all indigenous Zapotec-speaking people.

The Valley of Oaxaca's vibrant and prosperous native presence flows from a fortunate turn of history. During the mid-1800s, Mexico's Laws of the Reform forced the sale of nearly all church lands throughout the country. In most parts of Mexico, rich Mexicans and foreigners bought up much of these holdings, but in Oaxaca, isolated in Mexico's far southern region, there were few rich buyers, so the land was bought at very low prices by the local people, most of them indigenous farmers. Moreover, after the Revolution of 1910-1917, progressive federal-government land-reform policies awarded many millions of acres of land to campesino communities, notably to Oaxaca Valley towns Teotitlán del Valle and Santa Ana del Valle, whose residents now conserve many thousand acres of rich valley fields and foothill forests.

Although the grand monuments, fascinating museums, good restaurants, and inviting handicrafts shops of Oaxaca City alone would be sufficient, a visit to Oaxaca is doubly rich because of the manifold wonders of the surrounding Valley of Oaxaca. The must-see highlights of the valley are the timeless Mitla and Monte Albán archaeological sites, the unique crafts—wool weavings, pearly black pottery, floral-embroidered blouses and dresses, and *alebrijes* (wood-carved animals)—and last but not least, the natural wonders at El Tule, Hierve El Agua, and San Sebastián de las Grutas.

You might even let the valley's *tianguis* (literally, "shade awnings" and synonymous with "native markets") guide you along your

Previous: Monte Albán; rugs for sale at the Zaachila *tianguis*. **Above:** a weaver at work in Teotitlán del Valle.

Highlights

★ **Santa María del Tule:** Townsfolk have literally built the town around their gigantic beloved El Tule tree, a cousin of the giant redwood trees of California (page 59).

★ **Teotitlán del Valle:** Fine wool carpets and hangings, known locally as *tapetes*, are the prized product of dozens of local family workshops and stores in this valley town (page 61).

★ **Mitla:** Explore the monumental plazas and columned buildings, handsomely adorned by a treasury of painstakingly placed Greca stone fretwork (page 65).

★ **Hierve El Agua:** The beautiful and the bizarre commingle here, where mineral water has pushed up from underground for centuries, creating an otherworldly landscape—with views to die for and an inviting mineral water pool to play in (page 68).

★ **San Bartolo Coyotepec:** Don't miss this small city where roadside workshops and a must-see museum display the pearly black pottery pioneered by celebrated potter Doña Rosa a generation ago (page 70).

★ **San Sebastián de las Grutas:** The idyllic setting is enough to please anyone. The presence of eerie caves only adds to the allure of this pristine hideaway in the foothills south of Oaxaca City (page 73).

★ **Zaachila:** Its monumental archaeological zone and riotously colorful *tianguis* (native market) make Zaachila a Thursday destination of choice in Oaxaca (page 75).

★ **Monte Albán:** Any day is a good day to visit Mesoamerica's earliest true metropolis, which to some still rules from its majestic mountain-top throne (page 77).

The Valley of Oaxaca

excursion path. Beneath the shadowed market canopies and the shops of Oaxaca's welcoming local people, you can look, select, and bargain for the wonderful handicrafts that travelers from all over the world come to the Valley of Oaxaca to buy.

PLANNING YOUR TIME

In four or five days, you can soak in the valley's highlights, perhaps scheduling your time according to market days.

Given the limited hotel choices in the Valley of Oaxaca and the relatively short distances (16-48 km/10-30 mi) from Oaxaca City, you can use your lodging in the city as a home base and take excursions from there to explore the valley.

For transportation, you can hire a guide for about $150-200 per day, which should include a car for 4-5 people; rent a car for around $50 per day; or use private tourist bus transportation for $10-20 per person per day. Each of these options can get you to most of the valley's highlights over three or four days. A fourth option, touring by local public bus from *camionera central segunda clase* (second-class bus station) is much cheaper, but it requires twice the time.

Some sights you won't want to miss are the archaeological zones of **Mitla,** on the east side, and **Monte Albán,** on the southwest side of the valley. Of the markets, the biggest are the **Tlacolula** Sunday market, the **Ocotlán** Friday market, the **Etla** Wednesday market, and the **Zaachila** Thursday market. Fascinating crafts villages along the way are **Teotitlán del Valle** (on the way to Tlacolula and Mitla); Santo Tomás Jalieza, San Martín Tilcajete, and **San Bartolo Coyotepec** (on the way back to Oaxaca City from Ocotlán); and the **Santa María Atzompa** pottery village (on the way to or from Monte Albán).

GETTING AROUND
Taxis, Buses, and Rental Cars

For Oaxaca Valley touring, the cheapest (but not quickest) option is to ride a bus from the west-side Abastos market *camionera central segunda clase* (second-class bus terminal). The buses run everywhere in the Valley of Oaxaca and beyond.

Get to the second-class bus terminal by walking one block south from the *zócalo*'s southwest corner, turn right at Las Casas, and keep walking about nine blocks. The big terminal is on the right.

More leisurely options include renting a car or riding a private tourist bus, or both. Get your car rental through either a travel agent or U.S. and Canadian toll-free car rental number before you leave home, or in Oaxaca locally: **Alamo** (at airport or Matamoros 203, tel. 951/503-3618, 951/501-2188, oaxalamo@hotmail.com); **Europcar** (at airport, or at Matamoros 101, tel. 951/143-8340, 951/5169305, toll-free tel. in Mexico 800/201-1111 or 800/201-2084); or **Economy Rent a Car** (at airport and at Cinco de Mayo 203, tel. 951/514-8534, toll-free tel. 800/002-5266, economyrentacar.com).

For economical private transportation-only tourist buses, a good bet is to go with **Viajes Turísticos Mitla** (at Hóstal Santa Rosa, Trujano 201, main office at Mina 501, tel. 951/516-6175 or 951/501-0220, fax 951/514-3152, vmitla@prodigy.net.mx). They offer many tours, including a guide and transportation, for small- or medium-size groups. Another good tour operator is **Santours** (Porfirio Díaz 102-C, tel. 951/514-1617, Morelos 802, tel. 951/514-0732, turismosantours.com), offering half-day, full-day, and private tours to all Oaxaca Valley destinations.

Guided Tours

Websites such as discover-Oaxaca.com or toursoaxaca.com and many others will provide a certified guide/driver, a comfortable van to ride in, and multiple tours to choose from. Shop the Internet, or, if you are already in Oaxaca, find the tour offices dotting the streets around the *zócalo* and in many hotel lobbies. There are also many individual guides; often your hotel or B&B can connect you with a bilingual guide.

One great guide guide option is **Judith**

Reyes López (Bed-and-Breakfast Oaxaca Ollin, Quintana Roo 213, tel./fax 951/514-9126, www.oaxacaollin.com), who operates through her Art and Tradition tours. Judith offers tours ranging from half-day city tours and whole-day Valley of Oaxaca archaeological and crafts-village outings to farther-reaching explorations of the art and architecture of venerable Dominican churches in the Mixteca. Contact her at her bed-and-breakfast, Oaxaca Ollin, a block north and a block east of the Centro Cultural de Santo Domingo.

On the other hand, travelers interested in the diverse natural world of Oaxaca might go with biologist Fredy Carrizal Rosales, owner-operator of **Tourism Service in Ecosystems** (tel. 951/515-3305, in-town cell tel. 044-951/164-1897, ecologiaoaxaca@yahoo.com.mx).

Customized explorations of Oaxaca's indigenous communities, traditions, and natural treasures are the specialty of native Zapotec guide Florencio Moreno, who operates **Academic Tours in Oaxaca** (Nieve 208A, Colonia Reforma, home tel. 951/518-4728, in-town cell tel. 044-951/510-2244, www.academictoursoaxaca.com). Florencio's tours reflect his broad qualifications: fluency in native dialects, historical knowledge, cultural sensitivity, personal connections with indigenous crafts communities, and expertise in wildlife-watching and identification. His excursions can be designed to last a day or a week and include any region of Oaxaca.

Commercial guided tours also provide a hassle-free means of exploring the Valley of Oaxaca. Travel agencies, such as **Viajes Turisticos Mitla** (at Hóstal Santa Rosa, Trujano 201, tel./fax 951/514-7800 or 951/514-7806, fax 951/514-3152), **Viajes Xochitlán** (M. Bravo 210A, tel. 951/514-3271 or 951/514-3628, www.xochitlan-tours.com.mx, 9am-2pm and 4pm-7pm Mon.-Sat.), and others, offer such tours for about $12-15 for a half day and $18-20 for a full day, meals and entry fees not included.

For an extensive list of guide recommendations, check at the **Oaxaca state tourist information office** (703 Av. Juárez, west side of El Llano park, tel. 951/516-0123, www.aoxaca.com, 8am-8pm daily).

The Textile Route

The host of colorful enticements along this path could tempt you into many days of exploring. For example, on Saturday you could head out, visiting the great El Tule tree and the weavers' shops in Teotitlán del Valle and continuing east for an overnight at Mitla. Next morning, explore the Mitla ruins, then return, stopping at the hilltop Yagul archaeological site and the Sunday market at Tlacolula.

One more day would allow time to venture past Mitla to the remarkable mountainside springs and limestone mineral deposits at Hierve El Agua. Stay longer and have it all: a two- or three-day stay in a colorful market town, such as Tlacolula, with a side trip to visit the textile market and community museum at Santa Ana del Valle.

Alternately, you could sign up for a tour that takes in El Tule, Teotitlán del Valle, Mitla, a *mezcal* distillery, and Hierve El Agua in a single long day with a stop for lunch. These six- to eight-hour tours run less than $20 per person (entry fees at sites and meals not included) and the driver-guides are usually fairly knowledgeable, cheerful, and bilingual.

EL TULE AND TLACOCHAHUAYA
★ Santa María del Tule

El Tule is a gargantuan Mexican *ahuehuete* (cypress) tree, possibly the most massive in Latin America, with a gnarled, house-sized trunk supporting a forest of limbs rising up

15 stories overhead. Down at ground level, the small town of Santa María del Tule has a crafts market, church, and topiary-bedecked plaza encircling this magnificent tree. Every year on October 7 the town celebrates El Tule's 2,000 plus years of existence by throwing a grand fiesta. This is an awe-inspiring tree, well worth the 14-kilometer (nine mi) trip east from Oaxaca City on Highway 190.

Tlacochahuaya

At San Jerónimo Tlacochahuaya, seven kilometers (four mi) east of El Tule, stands the 16th-century Templo y Ex-Convento de San Jerónimo, built by Dominican friars and their indigenous acolytes over a few decades beginning in 1586. If you love old churches, by all means drop in for an hour and have a look around. This recently-restored church houses several exquisite paintings, especially the group depicting the legend of the Virgin of Guadalupe. You'll find the town most interesting in the last week of September, when the annual fiesta takes places, climaxing on September 30, the feast day of San Jerónimo.

DAINZU AND LAMBITYECO ARCHAEOLOGICAL SITES

Among the several Valley of Oaxaca buried cities, Dainzu and Lambityeco, both beside Highway 190, are the most accessible. Dainzu comes first, on the right, about nine kilometers (six mi) east of El Tule. Though there is not that much to actually see, and nothing dramatic at all, these two sites are relatively easy to get to. The amateur or professional archaeologist will assuredly find them interesting, the rest of us less so. They're worth a stop if you are in a rental car or on a private tour. They are not on most of the tour itineraries.

Dainzu

Dainzu ("Hill of the Organ Cactus" in Zapotec; Hwy. 190, no phone, 10am-5pm daily, $3) spreads over an approximate half-mile square, consisting of a partly restored ceremonial center surrounded by clusters of unexcavated mounds. Beyond that, on the west side, a stream runs through fields, which at Dainzu's apex (around AD 300) supported a town of about 1,000 inhabitants.

cypress tree El Tule

Town Names

Town names in Oaxaca (and in Mexico) generally come in two pieces: an original native name accompanied by the name of the town's patron saint. Very typical is the case of San Jerónimo Tlacochahuaya, a sleepy but famous little place. Combining both the saint's name (here, San Jerónimo) and the native name (here, Tlacochahuaya) often makes for very unwieldy handles; so, many towns are known only by one name, usually the native name. Thus, in the west side of the Valley of Oaxaca, San Jerónimo Tlacochahuaya, Santa María del Tule, Tlacolula de Matamoros, and San Pablo Villa de Mitla, for example, are commonly called Tlacochahuaya, El Tule, Tlacolula, and Mitla, respectively.

Nevertheless, sometimes a town's full name is customarily used. This is especially true when a single name—such as Etla, northwest of Oaxaca City—identifies an entire district, and thus many towns, such as San Agustín Etla, San Sebastián Etla, and San José Etla, must necessarily be identified with their full names. In this book, although we may mention the formal name once on a map or in the text, we generally conform to local, customary usage for town names.

Lambityeco

Ten kilometers (six mi) farther, **Lambityeco** (Hwy. 190, no phone, 10am-5pm daily) is on the right, a few miles past the Teotitlán del Valle side road. The excavated portion, only about 100 square yards, is a small but significant part of Yegui ("Small Hill" in Zapotec), a large buried town dotted with hundreds of unexcavated mounds covering about half a square mile. The name "Lambityeco" may derive from the Arabic-Spanish *alambique*, the equivalent of the English "alembic," or distillation or evaporation apparatus. This would explain the intriguing presence of more than 200 local mounds. It's tempting to speculate that they are the remains of *cujetes*, raised leaching beds still used in Mexico for concentrating brine, which workers subsequently evaporate into salt.

★ TEOTITLÁN DEL VALLE

Teotitlán del Valle (pop. 5,000), 14 kilometers (nine mi) east of El Tule, at the foot of the northern Sierra, means "Place of the Gods" in Nahuatl; before that, it was known, appropriately, as Xa Quire (shah KEE-ray), or "Foot of the Mountain," by the Zapotecs who settled it at least 2,000 years ago (by archaeologists' estimate).

Present-day Teotitlán people are relatively well off, not only from sales of their renowned *tapetes* (wool rugs), but from their rich communal landholdings. Besides a sizable swath of valley-bottom farmland and pasture, which every Teotitlán family is entitled to use, the community owns a dam and reservoir and a small kingdom of approximately 100,000 acres of sylvan mountain forest and meadow, spreading for about 32 kilometers (20 mi) along the Valley of Oaxaca's lush northeastern foothills.

Textile Shops

Nearly every Teotitlán house is a mini-factory where people card, spin, and color wool, often using hand-gathered natural dyes. The weaving, on traditional handlooms, is the final, satisfying part of the process. The best weaving is generally the densest, typically packing in about 18 strands per centimeter (45 strands per inch); ordinary weaving incorporates about half that.

Visiting at least one workshop-store should be on your itinerary, and will be if you sign up for a tour. The artisans are well-versed at demonstrating their techniques for dye-making, spinning, and weaving, and the sales pitch that follows is generally low-key. These home workshops, once confined to the town center, now sprinkle nearly the entire mile-long entrance road.

Community Museum

Allow enough time to visit the community museum **Balaa Xtee Guech Gulal** (Hidalgo, tel. 951/524-4463, 10am-6pm Tues.-Sun., $3), whose name translates from the local Zapotec as "Shadow of the Old Town." It's on the north side of Hidalgo, about a block east of Juárez. Step inside and enjoy the excellent exhibits that illustrate local history, industry, and customs. One display shows the wool-weaving tradition (introduced by the Dominican padres), which replaced the indigenous cotton-weaving craft. Sources of some natural dyes—*cochinilla* (red cochineal), *musgo* (yellow moss and lichens), *anil* (dark blue indigo), and *quizache* bean (black)—are part of the exhibit.

Teotitlán Church

Built over an earlier Zapotec temple, the **Teotitlán church,** known as the Templo de la Precioso Sangre de Cristo (Church of the Precious Blood of Christ), contains many interesting pre-Columbian stones, which the Dominican friars allowed to be incorporated into its walls. Outside, behind the church, lies the reconstructed foundation corner, on the street, downhill, of the original **Zapotec temple.** Note the Zapotec stone fretwork, similar to the famous *Greca* (Grecian-like) remains at Mitla, 32 kilometers (20 mi) farther east.

Accommodations and Food

Sample Teotitlán's best at the traditional **Tlamanalli** restaurant (on Juárez, about a block south of Hidalgo, no phone, 1pm-4pm daily, possibly longer hours on Mon. and Thurs. when more people stop by, $5-10). Their menu of made-to-order Zapotec specialties, such as *sopa de calabaza* (squash soup) and *guisado de pollo* (chicken stew) is limited but highly recommended by Oaxaca City chefs.

Alternatively, for a lunch or early dinner treat, stop at **Restaurant El Patio** (Hwy. 190, 1.2 km/0.8 mi east of the Teotitlán entrance road, tel. 951/514-4889, 10am-6pm Tues.-Sun.). The restaurant centers around an airy patio, decorated by antique country furniture and a fetching gallery of scenes from the 1940s-era films of the Mexican Golden Age of cinema. The ambience is wonderful; the food, which can be inconsistent, consists of tasty traditional Oaxacan dishes, such as *ensalada Oaxaqueña* and Zapotec soup.

Getting There

You can go to Teotitlán del Valle by car, tour,

woven rugs on display in a shop in Teotitlán del Valle

taxi, or bus. Drivers: Simply turn left from Highway 190 at the signed Teotitlán del Valle side road, 14 kilometers (nine mi) east of El Tule. By bus: Ride a **Fletes y Pasajes** Tlacolula- or Mitla-bound bus from the *camionera central segunda clase* (in Oaxaca City by the Abastos market at the end of Las Casas, past the *periférico* west of downtown).

TLACOLULA

The Zapotec people who founded **Tlacolula** (pop. 15,000, 38 km/24 mi east from Oaxaca City) around AD 1250 called it Guichiibaa ("Place Between Heaven and Earth"). Besides its beloved church and chapel and famous Sunday market, Tlacolula is also renowned for *mezcal,* a Tequila-like alcoholic beverage distilled from the fermented hearts of maguey, also known as agave. *Mezcal* is Oaxaca's obsession, pride, and joy, and getting out to see where it is made is now a big part of the Oaxaca experience—and well worth it, since you not only get to witness the process, you can try a few samples of the smoky brew. Get a good free sample at the friendly **Pensamiento shop** (Juárez 9, tel. 951/562-0017, 9am-7pm daily), about four blocks from the highway gasoline station (along Juárez) toward the market.

Just before the market, take a look inside the main town church, the 1531 **Parroquia de la Virgen de la Asunción.** Although its interior is distinguished enough, the real gem is its attached chapel, **Capilla del Señor de Tlacolula,** which you enter from the nave of the church. Every inch of the chapel's interior gleams with sculptures of angels and saints, paintings, and gold scrollwork.

The big gate bordering the church grounds leads you to the Tlacolula **market.** One of Oaxaca's biggest and oldest, the Tlacolula market draws tens of thousands from all over the Valley of Oaxaca every Sunday. Wander around and soak it all in—the diverse crowd of buyers and sellers, and the equally manifold galaxy of merchandise.

For food and accommodations, try the basic but clean downtown Tlacolula lodging, the **Hotel and Restaurant Calenda** (Juárez 40, tel. 951/562-0660, entrées $3-8, lodging $20 s or d, $30 t). They offer about 30 rooms with fans and hot-water shower-baths in three floors around an interior restaurant courtyard. Their restaurant serves a wholesome country menu that, although specializing in *barbacoa pollo, chivo,* or *borrego* (barbecue chicken, goat, or lamb), offers many more hearty choices, such as

A shop owner explains the creation of natural dyes for rugs in Teotitlán del Valle.

Mezcal Magic

Hundreds of small distilleries produce and market mezcal in Oaxaca.

"Para todo mal, mezcal, y para todo bien también" ("for everything bad, *mezcal;* for everything good, the same"). This saying reflects the integral role *mezcal* plays in Oaxacan culture. With agave growing in hundreds of small-scale family plots, *mezcal* is a modern-day cultural phenomenon in Oaxaca—one with deep historical roots. Some argue (especially after eating the worm found at the bottom of many bottles of *mezcal*) that this liquor has psychedelic properties. It does not, and bears no chemical or psychic relationship to mescaline, which comes from a mushroom, or peyote, which comes from a different sort of cactus. *Mezcal* is merely a flavorful and potent form of alcohol.

Mezcal has been the "national" drink of the state of Oaxaca for centuries. Like its more famous cousin, tequila (tequila is a *mezcal*, *mezcal* is not a tequila), *mezcal* is made from the maguey, a.k.a. agave, cactus, but there is a huge difference: tequila is always made from a single distinct species of agave, while *mezcal* can be made from any of the 30 or so types of agave (most commonly it is made from the one called Espadin). Although it can be drunk new, rested, or aged, just like tequila, the flavor is smokier and more complex. It is not recommended for mixed drinks, although various iterations of *mezcal* martinis are popping up on restaurant menus in Mexico and the United States. The Oaxacans generally savor it straight up, drinking slowly, biting into a slice of fresh orange coated with a combination of *sal gusano* (salt, chile, and freshly ground worms) after each sip.

Mezcal-making follows a series of steps that have been the same for centuries. Though perhaps more mechanized than in the past, it is mostly the same hands-on, handmade operation: using machetes, *mezcaleros* cut the plants, weighing up to 90 pounds, by hand. They hack the leaves off, leaving the heart, or piña, which does resemble an oversized pineapple. The piñas are cooked for three days, in a pit oven over piles of hot rocks. Hence the smoky flavor. The piñas are then crushed and mashed, and their juices are left to ferment in vats or barrels of water. In time, it is bottled, and you have *mezcal: blanco, reposado,* or *añejo* (white/young, rested, or aged, respectively).

For a serious trip into the world of Oaxacan *mezcal*, take a *mezcal* tour with Alvin Starkman, author of a book on the subject. You can reach him to set up a tour or explore the world of *mezcal* online through http://www.oaxaca-mezcal.com.

pork chops, spaghetti, eggs, fish, and chiles rellenos.

The Sunday market is usually "bundled" with a tour that might include, say, El Tule and Mitla, in a half day, or some other combination, with a well-spent hour or so dedicated to exploring the market. Ask around at any of the many tour offices in Oaxaca City to find a tour that best suits your interests, be they markets, churches, or archaeology; most of the organized tours out of Oaxaca City offer a sampling of all three.

YAGUL ARCHAEOLOGICAL ZONE

The remains of **Yagul** (Zapotec for "Old Tree"; 45 km/28 mi east of Oaxaca City, just north of Hwy. 190, no phone, 10am-5pm daily, $3) preside atop their volcanic hilltop. Although only 12 kilometers (7.5 mi) from Mitla and sharing architectural details, such as Mitla's famous *Greca* (Grecian-like) fretwork, the size and complexity of Yagul's buildings suggest that Yagul was an independent city-state in its own right. Locals call the present ruin the Pueblo Viejo (Old Town) and remember it as the forerunner of the present town of Tlacolula. Archaeological evidence, which indicates that Yagul was occupied for about a thousand years, at least until around AD 1100 or 1200, bears them out.

One of Yagul's major claims to fame is its **Palace of Six Patios,** actually three nearly identical but separate complexes of two patios each. In each patio, rooms surround a central courtyard.

South of the palace sprawls Yagul's huge **ball court,** the second largest in Mesoamerica, shaped in the characteristic Oaxaca I configuration. Southeast of the ball court is Patio 4, consisting of four mounds surrounding a courtyard. A boulder sculpted in the form of a frog lies at the base of the east mound.

★ MITLA

The ruins at **Mitla** (Hwy. 176, about 57 km/35 mi east of Oaxaca City, no phone, 8am-5pm daily, $5) are a "must" for Valley of Oaxaca sightseers. Mitla (Liobaa in Zapotec, the "Place of the Dead") flowered late, reaching a population of perhaps 10,000 during its apex around AD 1350. It remained occupied and in use for generations after the conquest.

Exploring the Site

In a real sense, Mitla lives on. The ruins coincide with the present town of **San Pablo**

Mitla's striking architectural style is both Zapotec and Mixtec.

Mitla

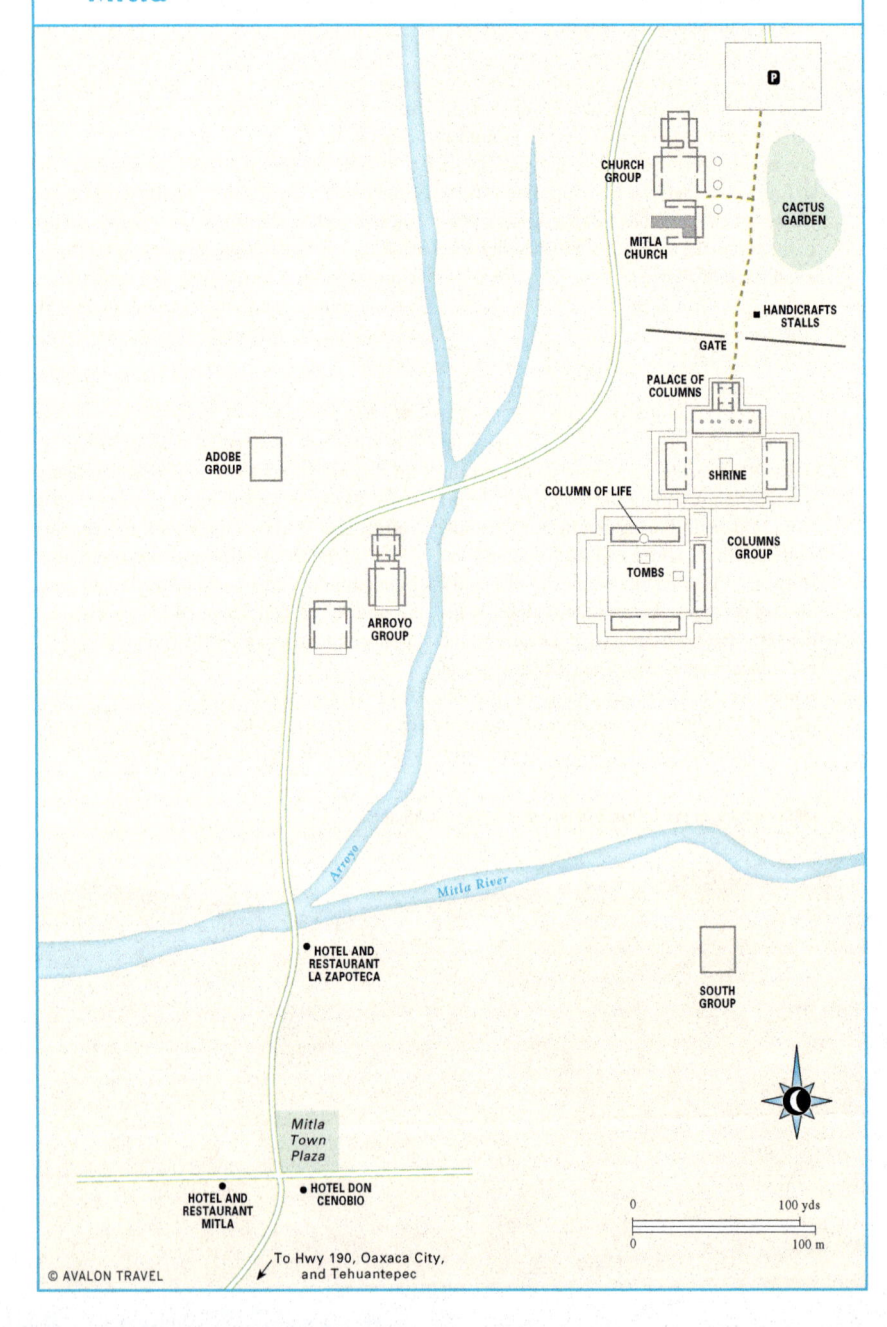

Villa de Mitla, whose main church occupies the northernmost of five main groups of monumental ruins. Virtually anywhere archaeologists dig within the town they hit remains of the myriad ancient dwellings, plazas, and tombs that connected the still-visible landmarks.

On the main entrance path, continue past the tourist market and through the gate to the **Columns Group.** Of the five ruins clusters, the best preserved is the fenced-in Columns Group. Its exploration requires about an hour. Inside, two large patios, joined at one corner, are each surrounded on three sides by elaborate apartments. A shrine occupies the center of the first patio. Just north of this stands the **Palace of Columns,** the most important of Mitla's buildings. It sits atop a staircase, inaccurately reconstructed in 1901.

The interesting **Church Group** (marked by the monumental columns that you pass first on your right after the parking lot) is on the far north side of the Palace of Columns. Builders used the original temple stones to erect the church here.

Shopping

Instead of making handicrafts, Mitla residents concentrate on selling them, mostly at the big **handicrafts market** adjacent to the archaeological zone parking lot. Here, you can sample from a concentrated all-Oaxaca assortment, especially textiles: cotton *huipiles,* wool hangings and rugs, onyx animals and chess sets, fanciful *alebrijes* (wooden animals), and leather huaraches, purses, belts, and wallets.

Accommodations and Food

Restaurant La Choza (Carretera Oaxaca-Mitla km 3.5, tel. 225-7878, $10 lunch buffet, credit cards accepted), on the right side of the road going in to Mitla, is where many tour bus operators bring their troops of passengers for lunch between destinations. The dining room is large, airy, and busy, and the food is done buffet style, with myriad options available in big pots and trays along the side and back walls. While some of the cooked items are overcooked for obvious reasons, there are plenty of fresh fruits and vegetables available, and enough good main courses—just about anything and everything that says Oaxacan or Mexican cuisine is here in some form or other—to make the price seem reasonable since you will likely be tanking up for a long day, between visiting Teotitlán and driving to Mitla and/or Hierve El Agua.

Alternatively, closer to the archaeological

The town's Catholic church was built atop a pyramid at Mitla.

zone, try the family-run ★ **Hotel and Restaurant La Zapoteca** (Cinco de Febrero 12, tel. 951/568-0026, ivettsita_revelde@hotmail.com, restaurant 8am-6pm daily; lodging $15 s, $20 d, $27 t), on the right just before the Río Mitla bridge. The spic-and-span restaurant, praised by locals for "the best mole negro and chiles rellenos in Oaxaca," is fine for meals, and the 20 clean, reasonably priced rooms, with hot water, in-house Internet, and parking, are good for an overnight.

Getting There

Bus travelers can get to Mitla from Oaxaca City by Fletes y Pasajes or Oaxaca-Istmo bus from the *camionera central segunda clase* (second-class bus station). Drivers get here by forking left from main Oaxaca Highway 190, at the big Mitla sign, onto Highway 176. Continue about 3.2 kilometers (two mi) to the Mitla town entrance, on the left. Turn left, and head straight past the town plaza. Continue across the bridge over the (usually dry) Río Mitla, and, after about 1.6 kilometers (one mi), arrive at the archaeological site.

This destination is included in countless half- and full-day tours out of Oaxaca City, and most of the drivers and/or guides are fairly well-versed in Mitla lore. Half-day tours generally run 10am-2pm, full days 10am-6pm, with meals and entry fees not included in the $12-15 half-day, $15-18 full-day tour fee. If you want to look at some options in advance of traveling, check the website go-oaxaca.com, which offers all the basic tours out of Oaxaca City into the Valley. There's no need to reserve, however: there are plenty of tour packages available once you're on the ground in Oaxaca.

★ HIERVE EL AGUA

Although the name of this place translates as boiling water, the springs that seep from the side of a limestone mountain less than an hour's drive east of Mitla aren't hot. Instead, they are loaded with minerals. These minerals over time have built up into rock-hard deposits, forming great algae-painted slabs in level

the mineral waterfall at Hierve El Agua

spots and, on steep slopes, accumulating into what appear to be grand frozen waterfalls.

The Springs

At **Hierve El Agua** (no phone, 9am-6pm daily, $2) the first thing you'll see after passing the entrance gate is a lineup of snack and curio stalls at the cliff-side parking lot. A trail leads downhill to the main spring, which bubbles from the mountainside and trickles into a huge basin that the operators have dammed as a swimming pool. Bring your bathing suit: if the weather is good it's a wonderful place for a dip.

Part of Hierve El Agua's appeal is the panoramic view of mountain and valley. On a clear day, you can see the tremendous massif of Zempoatepetl (saym-poh-ah-TAY-pehtl), the grand holy mountain range of the Mixe people, rising above the eastern horizon.

From the ridge-top park, agile walkers can hike farther down the hill, following deposits curiously accumulated in the shape of miniature limestone dikes that trace the mineral water's downhill path. Soon you'll glimpse a towering limestone formation, like a giant petrified waterfall, appearing to ooze from the cliff downhill straight ahead, on the right.

Hikers can also enjoy following a *sendero peatonal* (footpath) that encircles the entire zone. Start your walk from the trailhead beyond the bungalows or at the other end, at the cliff edge between the parking lot and the entrance gate. Your reward will be an approximately one-hour, self-guided tour, looping downhill past the springs and the great frozen rock cascades and featuring grand vistas of the gorgeous mountain and canyon scenery along the way.

Accommodations and Food

The Hierve El Agua tourist ★ **cabañas ecoturísticas** ($10 pp, $40 up to six people in a bungalow) are fine for a restful one-night stay. There are several clean and well-maintained housekeeping bungalows, with shower-baths and hot water, as well as bungalows for up to groups of six, with refrigerator, stove, and utensils. For information about cabaña reservations, contact the **Oaxaca state tourist information office** (Av. Juárez 703, west side of El Llano park, tel. 951/516-0123, www.aoxaca.com, 8am-8pm daily).

For food, you can bring and cook your own in your bungalow or rely upon the strictly local-style beans, carne asada (roast meat), tacos, tamales, and tortillas offered by the parking-lot food stalls.

Getting There

Get there by riding an Ayutla-bound Fletes y Pasajes bus east out of either Oaxaca City (departing from *camionera central segunda clase*) or from Mitla on Highway 179 just east of town. Get off at the Hierve El Agua side road, about 18 kilometers (11 mi) past Mitla. Continue the additional eight kilometers (five mi) by taxi or the local bus marked San Lorenzo.

Many tour operators operating out of Oaxaca City, such as **Verde Antequara Travel** (Murguía 100, tel. 951/514-8624) and **Monte Albán Tours** (Macedonio Alcalá 206-F, tel. 951/514-1385, 951/514-1976), include about a one- or two-hour visit to Hierve El Agua in their full-day tour packages, which run about $15-18 per person, meals and entry fees not included. The longish drive precludes its inclusion in half-day tours, but the spectacular scenery and the unusual nature of the site make this destination well worth visiting either on a tour or in a rental car should you have one.

natural mineral swimming pool at Hierve El Agua

The Crafts Route

Travelers who venture into the Valley of Oaxaca's long, south-pointing fingers, the Valleys of Zimatlán and Ocotlán, can discover a wealth of crafts, history, and architectural and scenic wonders. These are all accessible as day trips from Oaxaca City by car or combinations of bus and taxi. Most reachable are the renowned crafts villages of San Bartolo Coyotepec, San Martín Tilcajete, Santo Tomás Jalieza, and others along Highway 175, between the city and the colorful market town of Ocotlán (best to plan a visit to all on Friday, Ocotlán's market day; start at Ocotlán early and work your way north back to Oaxaca City). Another day, you can either continue farther south, off the tourist track, to soak in the feast of sights at the big market in Ejutla, or fork southwest, via Highway 131 through Zimatlán, to the idyllic groves, crystal springs, and limestone caves hidden around San Sebastián de las Grutas. The most renowned of the crafts villages have been included in quite a few tour itineraries, so if you dread driving, let someone else do it: shop around at any of the Oaxaca City-based tour companies previously listed, or ask at your hotel. You'll no doubt find one that includes at least a few of these destinations.

★ SAN BARTOLO COYOTEPEC

San Bartolo Coyotepec (Hill of the Coyote), on Highway 175, 23 kilometers (14 mi) south of Oaxaca City, is famous for its black pottery, the renowned *barro negro*. Sold all over Mexico, here it is available at the signed **Mercado de los Artesanias** market on the right and at a number of cottage factory shops (watch for signs) off the highway, scattered along the left (east side) of Calle Juárez, marked by a big Doña Rosa sign. Doña Rosa, who passed away in 1980, pioneered the technique of crafting lovely, big, round jars without a potter's wheel. With their local clay, Doña Rosa's descendants and neighbor families regularly turn out acres of glistening black

Mercado de los Artesanias, San Bartolo Coyotepec

Building Churches

Although European architects designed nearly all of Mexico's colonial-era churches, embellishing them with Old-World Gothic, Renaissance, baroque, and Moorish decorations, native artists blended their own geometric, floral, and animal motifs. The result was a hybrid that manifested in intriguing variations all over Mexico. This was especially true in Oaxaca, where faithful droves worship before gilded altars and flowery ceilings built and decorated by their long-gone ancestors. Local materials further distinguish Oaxacan churches from others in Mexico. The spectrum of soft pastels of local *cantera* volcanic stone, from yellow through gray, including green in Oaxaca City, marks Oaxacan walls and facades.

THE LAYOUT

Mexican church design followed the Egypto-Greco-Roman tradition of its European models. Basically, architects designed their churches beginning with the main space of the nave, in the shape of a box, lined with high lateral windows. Depending on their origin and function, the churches fit into three basic groups: the monk's *convento* (monastery or convent); the bishop's *catedral* (cathedral); and the priest's *templo* or *parroquia* (parish church).

In Oaxaca, faced with the constant threat of earthquakes, the Dominican padres built massively thick walls supported on the exterior with ponderous buttresses. Key elements were naves, with or without *cruceros* (transepts), cross spaces separating the nave from the altar, making the church layout resemble a Christian cross. They placed the *coro* (choir) above and just inside the entrance arch.

At the opposite, usually east (or sunrise) end of the church, builders sometimes extended the nave beyond the transept to include a *presbiterio* (presbytery), which was often lined with seats where church officials presided. The building ended past that at the *ábside* (apse), the space behind the altar, frequently in semi-circular or half-octagonal form. Within the apse rose the gilded *retablo* (retable or altarpiece), adorned with sacred images, attended by choirs of angels and cherubs.

THE FACADE

Outside, in front, rises the *fachada* (facade), sometimes in a uniform style, but just as often with a mixture of Renaissance, Gothic, and baroque, with some *mujedar* (Moorish) worked into the mix. A proliferation of columns nearly always decorates Oaxacan church facades, from the classic *Toscano, Dórico, Jónico,* and *Corintio* (Etruscan, Doric, Ionic, and Corinthian) pillars to spiraled *Salomónico* (Solomonic) barber's poles and bizarre *estipites.*

CONVENTS

The monastery- or convent-style churches included, in addition to all of the above, living and working quarters for the members of the order, typically built around a columned patio called the *claustro* (cloister). A corridor through an arched *portería* (porch) adjacent to the nave usually leads to the cloister, from which monks and nuns could quickly reach the dining hall, or *refectorio* (refectory), and their private rooms, or *celdas* (cells).

The Oaxacan missionary fathers always designed their churches with an eye to handling the masses of natives whom they hoped to convert. Padres included an *atrio* (atrium), a large exterior courtyard in front of the facade, for the potential large audience. For the partly initiated natives, they often built a *capilla abierta* (open chapel) on one side of the atrium. Conversions also occurred at smaller open chapels called *pozas,* built at the corners of the atrium.

plates, pots, bowls, trees of life, and fetching animals for very reasonable prices.

San Bartolo Museum

Across the highway from the town church, on the town plaza's southern flank, stands the large, new **Museo Estatal de Arte Popular** (Plaza Principal, tel. 951/551-0036, 10am-6pm Tues.-Sun., $4). Although the main event is a fine exposition of San Bartolo Coyotepec's famed black pottery, the museum also exhibits a surprisingly innovative range of some of the best crafts that the Valley of Oaxaca offers. Besides Doña Rosa's classic pearly-black examples, a host of other pieces—divine angels, scowling bandidos, fierce devils—reveal the remarkable talent of Doña Rosa's generation of students and followers.

SAN MARTÍN TILCAJETE AND SANTO TOMÁS JALIEZA

San Martín Tilcajete (teel-kah-HAY-tay; Hwy. 175, not far north of the Hwy. 131 fork), about 37 kilometers (21 mi) south of Oaxaca City, is a prime source of *alebrijes,* fanciful wooden creatures occupying the shelves of crafts stores the world over. Both it and **Santo Tomás Jalieza** (Hwy. 175, south of the Hwy. 131 fork), a mile or two farther south, can be visited as a pair on any day.

The label *alebrije,* a word of Arabic origin, implies something of indefinite form, and that certainly characterizes the fanciful animal figurines that a generation of Oaxaca woodcarvers has been crafting from soft copal wood. Dozens of factory-stores sprinkle San Martín Tilcajete.

Santo Tomás Jalieza, on the other hand, is known as the town of embroidered *cinturones* (belts). Women townsfolk, virtually all of whom practice the craft, concentrate all of their selling in a single, many-stalled **market** (Centro de Artesanias, Plaza Principal, no phone, 9am-5pm daily) in the middle of town.

A couple of local restaurants are recommended. Although it caters to the tourist crowd, the food is good and innovative at **Restaurant Azucena** (on the Tilcajete entrance road, tel. 951/524-9227). On the other hand, for truly rustic, ranch-style ambience, complete with old wagon wheels, wooden picnic-style tables, and plenty of savory barbeque, stop by **Restaurant Huamuches** (on the highway, by the Santo Tomás Jalieza entrance road, no phone).

OCOTLÁN

The main **Ocotlán** attraction is the huge **Friday market** (Centro district, between the central park and temple). Beneath a riot of colored awnings, hordes of merchandise—much modern stuff, but also plenty of old-fashioned goodies—load a host of tables and street-laid mats.

Since markets are best in the morning, you should make Ocotlán your first Friday stop. Drivers could get there by heading straight south out of the city, arriving in Ocotlán by mid-morning. Spend a few hours, then begin your return in the early afternoon, stopping at the sprinkling of crafts villages along the road back to Oaxaca. Bus travelers could hold to a similar schedule by riding an early Autobuses Estrella del Valle, Autotransportes Oaxaca-Pacífico, or Choferes del Sur from the *camionera central segunda clase* (second-class bus station), then returning, in steps, by bus, or more quickly by taxi, stopping at the crafts villages along the way.

Casa de Cultura Rudolfo Morales

During the 1980s and 1990s, Ocotlán came upon good times, largely due to the late Rudolfo Morales, the internationally-celebrated, locally-born artist who dedicated his fortune to improving his hometown. The Rudolfo Morales Foundation has been restoring churches and other public buildings, reforesting mountainsides, and funding self-help and educational projects all over Ocotlán and its surrounding district. The bright colors of the plaza-front *presidencia municipal* and the big church nearby

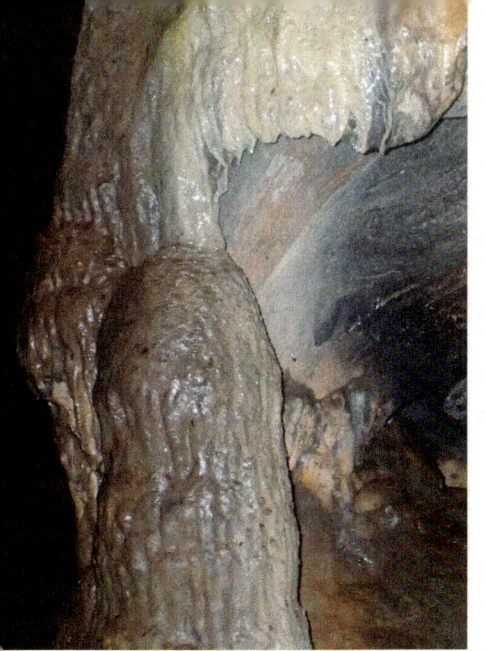

the cave at San Sebastián de las Grutas

result from the good works of Rudolfo Morales.

The Morales Foundation's local efforts radiate from the **Casa de Cultura Rudolfo Morales** (Morelos 108, tel. 951/571-0198, 9am-2pm and 5pm-8pm Mon.-Fri., 9am-3pm Sat.), in the yellow-painted mansion three doors north from the Ocotlán plaza's northwest corner. In the Casa de Cultura's graceful, patrician interior, the Morales family and staff manage the foundation's affairs, teach art and computer classes, and sponsor community events.

The foundation staff welcomes visitors. For advance information, contact the foundation's **headquarters in Oaxaca City** (Murguia 105, between Macedonio Alcalá and Cinco de Mayo, tel. 951/514-2324 or 951/514-0910, www.artedeoaxaca.com, 11am-3pm and 5pm-8pm Mon.-Sat.).

Templo de Santo Domingo

Local people celebrate Rudolfo Morales's brilliant restoration of their beloved 16th-century **Templo de Santo Domingo** (Juarez, next to the park). Gold and silver from the infamous Santa Catarina Minas (mines), in the mountains east of Ocotlán, financed the church's initial construction. When overwork and disease tragically decimated the local native population by around 1600, the mines were abandoned, and work on the church stopped. Although eventually completed over the succeeding three centuries, it had slipped into serious disrepair by the 1980s.

Fortunately, the Templo de Santo Domingo is now completely rebuilt, from its bright blue, yellow, and white facade to the baroque gold glitter of its nave ceiling.

Practicalities

Free yourself of the Friday downtown crowd at the rustic-chic restaurant **La Cabaña** (Hwy. 175, tel. 951/571-0201, 8am-7pm daily, $4-10), an open-air *palapa* by the *gasolinera* on the highway, at the north, Oaxaca, side of town.

If you decide to linger overnight in Ocotlán, the newish, clean, and modern **Hotel Rey David** (16 de Septiembre 248, tel. 951/571-1248, $13 s or d in one bed, $22 d or t in two beds) can accommodate you. The hotel offers about 20 comfortable, attractively decorated rooms. Find it on the south-side Highway 175 ingress-egress avenue, Avenida 16 de Septiembre, where it runs east-west, about three blocks east of the market and central plaza.

Do your money business at the Ocotlán **Banamex** (9am-4pm Mon.-Fri.), with ATM, on the north side of the town plaza.

★ SAN SEBASTIÁN DE LAS GRUTAS

It's hard not to fall in love with this idyllic hidden corner of the Valley of Oaxaca. The turnoff lies 73 kilometers (45 mi) south of Oaxaca City on Highway 131. After 0.4 kilometers (0.25 mi) toward the *grutas* (caves), the road becomes a gently winding, sylvan, creekside drive. The jade-green brook (muddy in the rainy season) gurgles downhill, pausing here and there in picture-perfect swimming holes.

Meanwhile, overhead, a regal host of towering, gnarled *sabinos* (bald cypress trees; *tules* or *ahuehuetes*) shades the creek, appearing every bit as ancient and grand as their northern cousins, the California redwoods. When you reach the edge of the village, you'll see farmers plowing their land with paired oxen, not tractors.

About 12 kilometers (seven mi) after the Highway 131 turnoff, and half a mile past San Sebastián de las Grutas village (pop. 900), you reach the cave area. The creek emerges clear and pristine, as if by magic, from beneath a big rock at the foot of a mountain.

Several hundred yards uphill—the climb is steep but paved and easy to manage—are the caves, which you can tour for a fee of about $2. A guide, armed with strong flashlights, will lead you on an easy, mostly level walk through the cave's several chambers, which vary from about 6 meters (20 ft.) to more than 60 meters (200 ft.) in height. The guide is used to receiving a tip of about $2 per person.

Practicalities

Spend the night in one of a dozen rustic wooden ***cabañas ecoturísticas*** (tel. 951/488-4640, $25 d, $30 t or q), with hot-water shower-bath, accommodating up to six people in an inviting, forest and meadow creekside setting at the foot of the trail leading to the cave.

The shady streamside park, furthermore, appears ripe for camping ($15), either in your tent or (self-contained) RV. For food and drinking water, bring your own or go to stores in the village. A small restaurant is included in the new buildings. It will open when and if there is enough business to sustain it.

Get there by bus via the Trans-Sol or Estrella Rojo del Sureste bus from the *camionera central segunda clase* (second-class bus station) next to the Abastos market on the southwest side of Oaxaca City. The Trans-Sol buses, some of which may (ask when you buy the ticket) go right to the caves, leave several times a day, beginning around 6am. The Estrella Rojo del Sureste may only drop you at the intersection, 13 kilometers (eight mi) from the caves. Take a taxi or *colectivo* van or truck from there. Drivers, follow Highway 131, a total of 76 kilometers (53 mi) south of Oaxaca City. Allow about two hours' driving time. In the reverse, north direction, the *grutas* (caves) are 190 kilometers (119 mi) north of Puerto Escondido.

tourist cabinas at Las Grutas, San Sebastián

SOUTHWEST SIDE
★ Zaachila

About 16 kilometers (10 mi) south of Oaxaca City, **Zaachila** (pop. 30,000), like Mitla, overlies the ruins of its ancient namesake city, which rose to prominence after the decline of Monte Albán. Although excavations have uncovered many Mixtec-style remains, historical records nevertheless list a number of Zapotec kings (including the greatest, Zaachila Yoo, for whom the town is named) who ruled Zaachila as a virtual Zapotec capital during the 14th and 15th centuries.

The big forested hill that rises north of the market plaza is topped by the **Zaachila pyramid** (no phone, 8am-5pm daily, $4). Several unexcavated mounds and courtyards dot the hill's north and south flanks.

In 1962, archaeologist Roberto Gallegos uncovered a pair of unopened tombs beneath the summit of the pyramid. They yielded a trove of polychrome pottery, gold jewelry (including a ring still on a left hand), and jade fan handles. Tomb 1 descends via a steep staircase to an entrance decorated with a pair of cat-motif heads. On the antechamber walls a few steps farther are depictions of owls and a pair of personages inscribed respectively with the name-dates 5-Flower and 9-Flower.

The Thursday *tianguis* (native market) is Zaachila's weekly main event. It spreads for blocks below the archaeological site and church. Thousands of Zapotec-speaking country people stream into town to buy, sell, gossip, flirt, and fill up with their favorite delicacies. If you're in the mood for food, wholesome country fare is available at the regiment of *fondas* in the roofed section of the market. Pork is a Zaachila ("Town of Pork") specialty, and any one of a small acre of pork stalls will be ready to barbeque a pork chop for you on the spot. Alternatively, enjoy lunch at the showplace ★ **Restaurant La Capilla** (tel. 951/528-6115, 7am-7pm daily, $5-10). Get there on foot or by asking your *moto-taxi* driver to let you off at La Capilla (kah-PEE-yah), on the main east-west Oaxaca ingress street, a few blocks west of the market.

By bus, get to Zaachila via **Autobuses de Oaxaca,** from the *camionera central segunda clase* (second-class bus station) in Oaxaca City, or by private tourist bus.

By car from Oaxaca City, head south from downtown to the *periférico*. Do not continue south via the airport Highway 131-175. Instead, from the *periférico* a block west of the airport-highway intersection (watch for the Monte Albán sign), follow the four-lane

Zaachila

boulevard that angles southwest, away from the *periférico,* across the Río Atoyac bridge. Just after crossing the bridge, do not continue straight ahead toward Monte Albán, but take the second left (south) onto the old (scenic route) Zaachila road, which also passes Cuilapan de Guerrero and Arrazola. These roads are in good condition and their signage is clear and easy to follow. You won't get lost out there.

Cuilapan de Guerrero and Arrazola

Southwest of Oaxaca City, on the old road between Zaachila and Arrazola, **Cuilapan de Guerrero** is famous for its elaborate but unfinished **Ex-Convento de Santiago** (Saint Jame, 9am-5pm daily). It's visible from the Oaxaca City-Zaachila Highway (via Xoxocotlan). This is where Vicente Guerrero, father of the Mexican republic, was infamously executed in 1831. Although construction began in 1535, the cost of the basilica and associated monastery began to balloon. In 1550, King Philip demanded humility and moderation of the builders, whose work was finally ended by a 1570 court ruling. The extravagances—the soaring, roofless basilica, magnificent baptismal font, splendid Gothic cloister, and elaborate frescoes—remain as national treasures. Extravagance has its value.

Arrazola, a few miles farther north, toward Oaxaca City, is one of the sources (along with San Martín Tilcajete) of the intricately painted *alebrijes* (ah-lay-BREE-hays)—fanciful wooden creatures that decorate the shelves of handicrafts shops all over Mexico and foreign countries. Bus travelers: Get here either by second-class bus or by tourist bus from Oaxaca City. Drivers: Turn west (left) onto signed Highway 145 a few miles north of Cuilapan de Guerrero or, traveling south, turn right 5.1 kilometers (3.2 mi) south of the Río Atoyac bridge in Oaxaca City. Pass through San Javier village and continue from the turn-off a total of five kilometers (three mi) to the Arrazola town plaza.

fruit and herbs for sale, Zaachila *tianguis*

Monte Albán and the Archaeological Route

★ MONTE ALBÁN

Monte Albán ranks among Mesoamerica's most spectacular ruined cities. Known in ancient times by its Zapotec name, Danni Dipaa, the site's present "Monte Albán" label was probably coined by a local Spaniard because of its resemblance to a similarly named Italian hilltop town.

The great city atop the hill reigned for at least 1,200 years, between 500 BC and AD 750, as the capital of the Zapotecs and the dominant force between Teotihuacán in the Valley of Mexico and the Maya kingdoms of the southeast. Archaeologists have organized the Valley of Oaxaca's history from 500 BC to the conquest into five periods, known as Monte Albán I-V. Over those centuries, the hilltop city was repeatedly reconstructed with new walls, plazas, and staircases, which, like layers of an onion, now overlie earlier construction.

Remains from Monte Albán Period I (500 BC-AD 1) reveal an already advanced culture, with gods, permanent temples, a priesthood, a written language, numerals, and a calendar. Sharply contrasting house styles indicate a differentiated, multilayered society. Monte Albán I ruins abound in graceful polychrome ceramics of uniquely Zapotec style.

Concurrent Olmec influences have also been found, notably in the buildings known as the Danzantes (Dancers), decorated with unique bas-reliefs similar to those unearthed along the Veracruz and Tabasco coasts.

The people who lived during Monte Albán Period II (AD 1-300), by contrast, came under heavy influence from Chiapas and Guatemala in the south. They built strange, ship-shaped buildings, such as Monte Albán's mysterious Building J, and left unique remains of their religion, such as the striking jade bat-god now on display in the Anthropology Museum in Mexico City.

Monte Albán reached its apex during the classical Period III (AD 300-800), attaining a population of perhaps 40,000 in an urban zone of about eight square kilometers (three sq mi), which spread along hilltops (including the El Gallo and Atzompa archaeological sites) west of the present city of Oaxaca.

Vigorous Period III leaders rebuilt the main hilltop complex as we see it today. Heavily influenced by the grand style of the Teotihuacán structures in the Valley of Mexico, the buildings were finished with handsome sloping staircases, corniced walls, monumental carvings, ball courts, and hieroglyph-inscribed stelae depicting gods, kings, and heroic scenes of battle.

In AD 800, Monte Albán, mysteriously cut off from the rest of Mesoamerica, was

steps at Monte Albán

Monte Albán

declining in population and power. By AD 1000, the city was virtually abandoned. The reasons—whether drought, disease, or revolt—and the consequent loss of the necessarily imported water, wood, salt, and food supplies remain an enigma.

During Periods IV and V, Mixtec peoples from the north invaded the Valley of Oaxaca. They warred with valley Zapotecs and, despite their relatively small numbers, became a ruling class in a number of valley city-states. The blend of Mixtec and Zapotec art and architecture sometimes led to new forms, especially visible at the west valley sites of Yagul and Mitla.

Exploring the Site

Visitors to **Monte Albán** (tel. 951/516-9770, 8am-5pm daily, entrance $5) enjoy a panoramic view of green mountains rising above the checkerboard of the Valley of Oaxaca. Allow at least two hours for your visit.

A good **guide** (about $10 pp for a two-hour tour) can certainly enhance your Monte Albán visit. Many are licensed by the authorities. You can often hire someone on the spot.

Past the visitor's center, as you enter the Main Plaza, north will be on your right, marked by the great **North Platform,** topped by clusters of temples. The **Ball Court** will soon appear on your left. Twenty-foot-high walkways circumscribe the sunken I-shaped playing field. This, like all Oaxacan ball courts, had no stone ring (for supposed goals), but rather four mysterious niches at the court's I-end corners.

The **Main Plaza,** 1,000 feet long and exactly two-thirds that wide, is aligned along a precise north-south axis. Probably serving as a market and civic/ceremonial ground, the monumentally harmonious Main Plaza was the Zapotec "navel" of the world.

Monte Albán's oldest monumental construction, the **Danzantes** building (surmounted by newer Building L, on the west side of the plaza between Buildings M and IV), dates from Period I. Its walls are graced with a host of personages, known commonly as the *danzantes* (dancers) from their oft-contorted postures—probably chiefs vanquished by Monte Albán's armies. Their headdresses, earplugs, bracelets, and necklaces mark them among the nobility, while glyphs around their heads identify each individual.

Building J (circa AD 1), one of the most remarkable in Mesoamerica, stands nearby in mid-plaza at the foot of the South Platform. Speculation has raged since excavators

Monte Alban's Building J

The Tragic Story of Princess Donaji

The fabled marriage of King Cosijoeza (koh-see-hoh-AY-zah) of the Zapotecs to Coyollicatzin (koh-yoh-yee-KAH-tseen), daughter of Emperor Moctezuma II of the Aztecs, around 1490, was a happy one. It resulted in five children, the youngest of whom was a charming little girl.

The king asked his soothsayers what their divinations told of his little daughter's future. They replied that her life would be filled with tragic events and that she would finally sacrifice herself for her people. The king, saddened by the news but happy that she would turn out to be so selfless, named her Donaji (Great Soul).

Earlier, Cosijoeza, who ruled the Zapotec Isthmus domains from his capital at present-day Tehuántepec, had been an uneasy ally of his old enemy, King Dzahuindanda (zah-ween-DAHN-dah) of the Mixtecs. In 1520, with the Aztec threat diminished by the Spanish invasion, Cosijoeza recklessly attacked the fierce Mixtecs, losing the initial battle and then nearly his life as the Mixtecs pressed their advantage.

However, the Spanish, in the person of Hernán Cortés's lieutenant, Francisco Orozco, soon imposed a Mixtec-Zapotec treaty in which Dzahuindanda received Princess Donaji as a hostage to guarantee the peace.

Having Donaji as a prisoner at Monte Albán (known as Danni Dipaa in those days) was not exactly an advantage to Dzahuindanda, for he suspected that she was as much a spy as a hostage. His guess was right. Donaji gleaned intelligence vital to the Zapotec counterattack her father Cosijoeza was planning. At the moment Dzahuindanda's forces were most vulnerable, she sent her father a secret message to attack, which he did, with complete success, except for one thing.

With the treaty broken, the outraged Mixtecs decided to do away with Donaji. They decapitated her and buried her body before her father could rescue her. Later, some Zapotecs found Donaji's remains on the bank of the Atoyac river. They were surprised to see a lovely violet wild iris blossoming from her blood. Even more surprising, they found the flower's roots growing around her head, which was without any sign of decomposition.

Three hundred years later, the Oaxaca government decided to honor the heroine who sacrificed herself for her people by adding an image of Donaji's head to the Oaxacan coat of arms, where it remains to the present day.

---

unearthed its arrow-shaped base generations ago. It is not surprising that Alfonso Caso, Monte Albán's original principal excavator, theorized it was an astronomical observatory (it does point in the direction of the setting sun at its winter solstice).

Aficionados can't resist claiming that Building J represents some other-worldly influence. They assert that the figure, visibly inscribed on the building's upper northwest corner, is an extraterrestrial wearing a space helmet. Expert professionals refute this with a more earthly explanation, that the figure simply represents a ball player wearing the customary protective leather helmet.

The **South Platform** affords Monte Albán's best viewing point, especially during the late afternoon. Starting on the right-hand, Palace-complex side, **Building II** has a peculiar tunnel on its near side, perhaps covertly used by priests for privacy or some kind of magical effect.

The South Platform itself is only marginally explored. Looters have riddled the mounds on its top side. Its bottom four corners were embellished by fine bas-reliefs, two of which had their engravings intentionally buried from view. You can admire the fine sculpture and yet-undeciphered Zapotec hieroglyphs on one of them, along with others, at the South Platform's plaza-edge west side.

On Monte Albán's northern periphery stand a number of tombs that, when excavated, yielded a trove of artifacts, now mostly housed in museums. Walking west from the

Northern Platform's northeast base corner, you will pass Mound X on the right. A few hundred yards farther comes the **Tomb 104** mound, presided over by an elaborate ceramic urn representing Cocijo, the Zapotec god of rain. Just north of this is **Tomb 172,** which has its skeletons and offerings left intact from when it was first opened.

Heading back along the northernmost of the two paths from Tomb 104, you will arrive at **Tomb 7** a few hundred feet behind the visitors center. Here, around 1450, Mixtec nobles removed the original eighth-century contents and reused the tomb, burying a deceased dignitary and two servants for the netherworld. Along with the bodies, they left a fabulous treasure in gold, silver, jade, alabaster, and turquoise, now visible at the museum at the Centro Cultural de Santo Domingo in Oaxaca City.

A few hundred feet toward town on the opposite side of the road from the parking lot is a trail leading past a small ball court to the Cerro de Plumaje (Hill of Plumage), site of **Tomb 105.** A magnificent entrance door lintel, reminiscent of those at Mitla, welcomes you inside. Past the patio, descend to the mural-decorated tomb antechamber. Inside the cruciform tomb itself, four figures walk in pairs toward a great glyph, flanked by a god and goddess, identified by their name-dates.

Visitors Center

The **Monte Albán Visitors Center** (tel. 951/516-9770, 8am-5pm daily) has an excellent museum, good café with airy terrace, and information counter. Also, a well-stocked **bookstore** (tel. 951/516-9180) offers many books on Mesoamerica, including travel, histories, art, and folklore books. In the bookstore, you might purchase a copy of the very useful *Guide to Monte Albán,* by Monte Albán's director, Neli Robles. You could also pick up a copy of the very authoritative, in-depth *Oaxaca, the Archaeological Record,* by archaeologist Marcus Winter.

Getting There

Get to Monte Albán economically and very conveniently by one of the several **tourist buses** run by **Hotel Rivera del Ángel** (Mina 518, tel. 951/516-6666) and **Viajes Turísticos Mitla** (Mina 501, tel. 951/516-5327). Find them three blocks south and four blocks west of the *zócalo* in Oaxaca City. The aptly-named **Monte Albán Tours** (tel. 951/514-1976, montealbantours.com) is one of many Oaxaca-based tour companies that

Santa María Atzompa is renowned for green-glazed pottery.

send a bus to Monte Albán every day, for a four-hour visit ($12 pp).

By car, get to Monte Albán via the most scenic route. Start from Oaxaca City's south side, at the *periférico,* past the end of southbound Calle M. Cabrera. Cross the *periférico,* then bear right and immediately cross over the Río Atoyac bridge. Continue ahead, following other Monte Albán signs, about eight kilometers (five mi), uphill, to Monte Albán.

Alternatively, get to Monte Albán by following Highway 190 northwest from downtown Oaxaca City. After three kilometers (two mi) from the city center, curve left, around the big monument and traffic circle, reversing your direction, then immediately turn right (west) and continue across the Río Atoyac bridge. Follow the signs about 10 more kilometers (six mi) uphill to Monte Albán.

SANTA MARÍA ATZOMPA

The present-day town of **Santa María Atzompa** (pop. 5,000) spreads somewhat chaotically over the western end of the greater Monte Albán archaeological complex, overlying hundreds of acres of unexplored ancient remains. The majority of modern Atzompans, however, have little time for the past. They are busy producing Atzompan pottery, famous all over Mexico and the world.

Along with their distinctive pottery creations—attractive emerald green-glazed cooking pots, bowls, baking dishes, plates—the local potters have turned to creating multicolored vases, some with artfully cut holes for placing dried or fresh flowers, as well as lily-adorned crosses, vases, plates, and red pottery, inscribed with fetching floral motifs. There is some beautiful stuff here, but also a lot of modern-day, made-for-tourists kitsch.

The work can be seen and purchased at the **Mercado de Artesanías** (Handicrafts Market, tel. 951/558-9232, or local cell tel. 044-951 516-5062, 9am-7pm daily), on the entrance road (right side) after a long initial line of private stores. Each of the *mercado* displays contains the name and address of the artist, whom you can contact nearby in town.

For lunch at the handicrafts market, try the adjacent ★ **Restaurant Patio** (no phone, 11am-6pm daily, $4). They offer a menu of many Mexican specialties, including a number of moles (with chicken) and the reliable favorite, chiles rellenos.

Photo Credits

Title page: cactus outside a Oaxacan cathedral © Kirsten Wardman; pg. 5 top and bottom: © Justin Henderson; pg. 7: © Justin Henderson; pg. 13: © Justin Henderson; pg. 14: © Justin Henderson; pg. 16: © Justin Henderson; pg. 17: © Justin Henderson; pg. 18: © Justin Henderson; pg. 20: © Justin Henderson; pg. 22: commons.wikimedia.org; pg. 32: © Justin Henderson; pg. 33: © Justin Henderson; pg. 41: © Justin Henderson; pg. 54 top and bottom: © Justin Henderson; pg. 55: © Justin Henderson; pg. 60: © Justin Henderson; pg. 62: © Justin Henderson; pg. 63: © Justin Henderson; pg. 64: © Justin Henderson; pg. 65: © Justin Henderson; pg. 67: © Justin Henderson; pg. 68: © Justin Henderson; pg. 69: © Justin Henderson; pg. 70: © Justin Henderson; pg. 73: © Justin Henderson; pg. 74: © Justin Henderson; pg. 75: © Justin Henderson; pg. 76: © Justin Henderson; pg. 77: © Justin Henderson; pg. 79: © Justin Henderson; pg. 81: © Justin Henderson

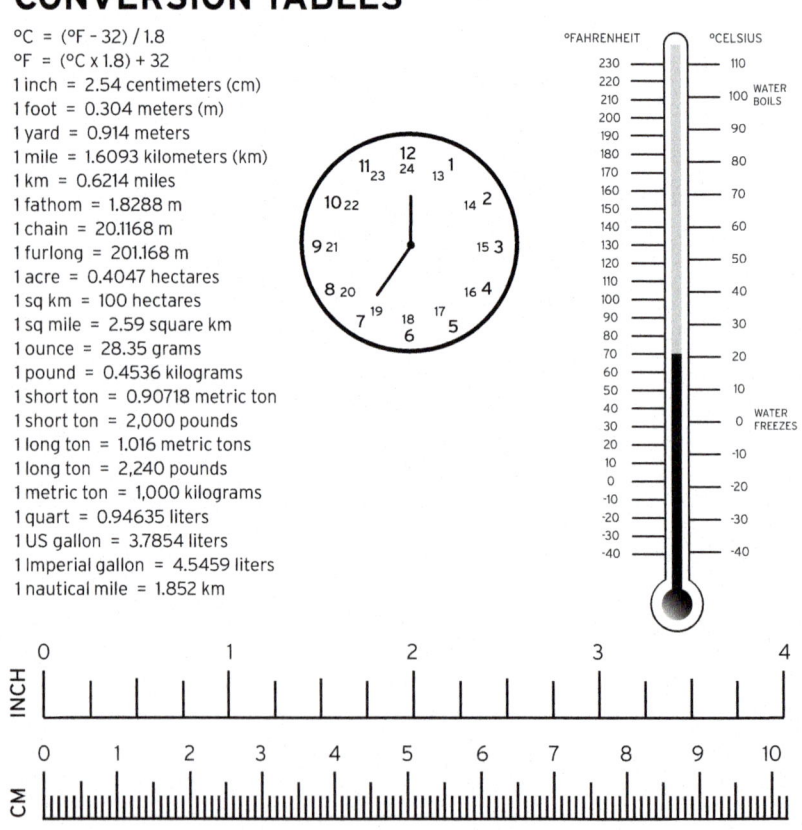

MAP SYMBOLS

Expressway	○ City/Town	✈ Airport
Primary Road	◉ State Capital	✈ Airfield
Secondary Road	⊛ National Capital	▲ Mountain
Unpaved Road	★ Point of Interest	✛ Unique Natural Feature
Feature Trail	• Accommodation	Waterfall
Other Trail	▼ Restaurant/Bar	▲ Park
Ferry	■ Other Location	Trailhead
Pedestrian Walkway	△ Campground	Skiing Area
Stairs		

Golf Course	Church
Parking Area	Gas Station
Archaeological Site	Glacier
	Mangrove
	Reef
	Swamp

CONVERSION TABLES

°C = (°F - 32) / 1.8
°F = (°C x 1.8) + 32
1 inch = 2.54 centimeters (cm)
1 foot = 0.304 meters (m)
1 yard = 0.914 meters
1 mile = 1.6093 kilometers (km)
1 km = 0.6214 miles
1 fathom = 1.8288 m
1 chain = 20.1168 m
1 furlong = 201.168 m
1 acre = 0.4047 hectares
1 sq km = 100 hectares
1 sq mile = 2.59 square km
1 ounce = 28.35 grams
1 pound = 0.4536 kilograms
1 short ton = 0.90718 metric ton
1 short ton = 2,000 pounds
1 long ton = 1.016 metric tons
1 long ton = 2,240 pounds
1 metric ton = 1,000 kilograms
1 quart = 0.94635 liters
1 US gallon = 3.7854 liters
1 Imperial gallon = 4.5459 liters
1 nautical mile = 1.852 km

MOON SPOTLIGHT OAXACA VALLEY
Avalon Travel
a member of the Perseus Books Group
1700 Fourth Street
Berkeley, CA 94710, USA
www.moon.com

Editor: Erin Raber
Series Manager: Kathryn Ettinger
Copy Editor: Naomi Adler Dancis
Graphics and Production Coordinator: Lucie Ericksen
Map Editor: Albert Angulo
Cartographer: Brian Shotwell

ISBN-13: 978-1-63121-102-7

Text © 2015 by Justin Hendersen and Avalon Travel.
Maps © 2015 by Avalon Travel.
All rights reserved.

Some photos and illustrations are used by permission and are the property of the original copyright owners.

Front cover photo: Monte Albán, Oaxaca © Michael Levy | Dreamstime.com
Printed in the United States

Moon Spotlight and the Moon logo are the property of Avalon Travel. All other marks and logos depicted are the property of the original owners. All rights reserved. No part of this book may be translated or reproduced in any form, except brief extracts by a reviewer for the purpose of a review, without written permission of the copyright owner.

All recommendations, including those for sights, activities, hotels, restaurants, and shops, are based on each author's individual judgment. We do not accept payment for inclusion in our travel guides, and our authors don't accept free goods or services in exchange for positive coverage.

Although every effort was made to ensure that the information was correct at the time of going to press, the author and publisher do not assume and hereby disclaim any liability to any party for any loss or damage caused by errors, omissions, or any potential travel disruption due to labor or financial difficulty, whether such errors or omissions result from negligence, accident, or any other cause.

About the Author

Justin Henderson

A native of Los Angeles, Justin Henderson spent much of his childhood and young adulthood surfing the California beaches. After his graduation from California State University, Northridge, his career took him to several locations across the country. He worked as an architectural journalist in New York City, and later moved to Seattle, where he worked as a freelance travel and design writer. It was in Seattle that he took up windsurfing, reviving his long-dormant surfing skills and his passion for the ocean. Justin then moved with his wife and daughter to Sayulita, 30 miles north of Puerto Vallarta. In his years living there, Justin learned to love Mexico even more than he did as a child when his family would vacation on Lake Chapala every summer.

Justin has written guidebooks on destinations ranging from Costa Rica to Los Angeles, and now Oaxaca, as well as six murder mysteries featuring a female travel writer and photographer which are set on Caribbean islands, in Costa Rica, and all over Mexico. He is currently working on the latest edition of *Moon Puerto Vallarta* as well as a memoir of his five years in Sayulita, tentatively called *Paradise on the Five Year Plan.*

Justin and his family recently returned to Seattle, though he considers anywhere near the Pacific to be home. His first purchase there was a new wetsuit.